Writing for Publication in Reading and Language Arts

James F. Baumann
University of Georgia

Dale D. Johnson
*Instructional Research and
Development Institute*

EDITORS

■ ■ ■ ■

International
Reading
Association
Newark,
Delaware
19714

The International Reading Association attempts, through its publications, to provide a forum for a wide spectrum of opinions on reading. This policy permits divergent viewpoints without assuming the endorsement of the Association.

Copyright 1991 by the
International Reading Association, Inc.

Library of Congress Cataloging in Publication Data

Writing for publication in reading and language arts/James F.
Baumann, Dale D. Johnson, editors.
    p.   cm.
Includes bibliographical references and index.
    1. Authorship—Marketing. 2. Publishers and publishing.
I. Baumann, James F. II. Johnson, Dale D.
PN161.w85 1991   91-13333
808'.02—dc20   CIP
ISBN 0-87207-365-3

Graphic design by *Boni Nash*

C o n t e n t s

Part One
Publishing in Journals, Newspapers, and Newsletters

Part Two
Publishing Materials for Children and Adolescents

Part Three

Publishing Textbooks and Professional Books

F o r e w o r d

Primo Levi, who liked to write about writing, once noted that "a piece of writing has all the more value and all the more hope of diffusion and permanence the better it is understood" (1989, p. 170).

The contributors to this volume offer a diverse set of perspectives on how we as writers can be better understood, whether we're writing an article about a teaching experience, a research book, or a children's story. The authors of this volume make an important assumption: we have stories to tell and knowledge to share with our colleagues. Each chapter provides important information about one of the specialized genres that make up writing related to reading and the language arts.

The volume is divided into three major sections: writing for journals and other periodicals, writing for children and adolescents, and writing instructional materials. Whatever the writer's purpose and intended audience, this volume provides detailed information about the contexts, processes, and products of publishing.

A truly literate community is one in which writers encourage other writers, share their knowledge and experiences, and read so that their voices might further develop. This volume makes an important contribution to the literate community. In a sense, the voices within *Writing for Publication in Reading and Language Arts* have much in common with the campfire round.

Someone starts the singing, others listen, appreciate, and grow familiar with the form and rhythm. Eventually, with encouragement, all members contribute their own voices, all worthy of a listen.

Peter Afflerbach
University of Maryland

Reference

Levi, P. (1989). *Other people's trades*. New York: Simon & Schuster.

Introduction

"**H**ow should you like to grow up a clever man and write books?" Oliver considered a little while.... "Well well," said the old gentleman, "Don't be afraid! We won't make an author of you while there is an honest trade to be learned, or brickmaking to turn to."
—from *Oliver Twist*, by Charles Dickens

Over lunch at IRA's Annual Convention in Anaheim, California, in May 1987, we reminisced about times past: when we first met in 1971, when Dale was an assistant professor at the University of Wisconsin and Jim was a graduate intern in the Native American Teacher Corps program; when we hooked up again six years later after Dale was a full professor and Jim had returned to Wisconsin to work on a Ph.D.; when we'd met subsequently at various professional meetings.

Our musings were mostly frivolous ("Remember, Dale, when you made me deliver your tuba to the Village Green tavern in Middleton for a performance of the Lost Century Jazz Band?"). But gradually the conversation drifted to more serious matters that included the writing and editing we had collaborated on since about 1979—the successful projects as well as those that bombed. We noted that despite having mentors in the field, much of what we learned about authoring came through experience, a good bit of it painful—the proverbial school of hard knocks.

Because IRA program proposal time was nigh, our ruminations turned toward what we might do at the 1988 convention in Toronto. Since our thoughts were focused on our successes and failures in professional publishing, we decided to conduct a pre-convention institute on the topic of writing for publication, thinking that others might learn from our experiences and those of our colleagues. After 15 minutes or so of scribbling notes on paper place mats and cocktail napkins, we had sketched out a program. The following spring in Toronto, we cochaired an institute on writing for publication. While organizing that meeting, we decided to coedit a volume on the same topic and submit it to IRA for possible publication. That is the history behind *Writing for Publication*.

Our purpose in assembling this book is to provide novice and experienced writers with a series of articles on the emotional, psychological, and nuts-and-bolts aspects of publishing professional and instructional materials in literacy education. We do not claim that this volume is comprehensive, although we believe that most all the major types of professional writing in reading and language arts education are addressed in some fashion. We also do not maintain that all articles are pragmatic pieces; neither the preconvention institute nor this book were conceived with that exclusive focus. Some articles address the passionate, emotional aspects of authoring—for example, Kameenui's chapter on writing articles for research journals, Livingston's chapter on authoring children's trade books, and Otto's chapter on authoring college textbooks.

> My passion was for the pen, the ecstasy of watching my scrawl cover the pages. It is the sort of trance saints speak of—a blissful heightened state in which you at once feel utterly alone and in harmony with the universe.
>
> —Erica Jong

On the other hand, many chapters provide concrete suggestions for writing different kinds of materials. Included in this category are Kruse's chapter on writing children's trade books, Howard and Canavan's chapter on preparing professional books and textbooks, Baumann's chapter on writing articles for practitioner journals, and Micklos's chapter on writing for newspapers and newsletters.

> The art of writing is the art of applying the seat of the pants to the seat of the chair.
>
> —Mary Heaton Vorse

Please recognize that we are not suggesting, by way of the more practical chapters, that writing of any sort is formulaic; it's not. Instead, we asked each contributor to tell us what it feels like to write, what works for her or him while writing, or both. As a result, the authors' voices are strong and clear in this work—a lesson we believe is one of the first to learn in acquiring the art of writing.

> Writing is both mask and unveiling.
>
> —E.B. White

We have organized *Writing for Publication* into three major sections. Part 1 deals with publishing in journals, periodicals, newspapers, and newsletters. Part 2 addresses writing materials for use with children and adolescents. Part 3 looks at the preparation of textbooks and professional books.

Part 1 includes six chapters on writing for various types of periodicals. The first two chapters deal with publishing in research journals. Samuels describes the process of conceiving of, designing, implementing, and reporting research in scholarly journals. He does this from the perspective of a journal editor—he formerly served as coeditor of *Reading Research Quarterly*. Kameenui provides insight into the process of inquiry an author must undertake in order to conceptualize and implement a successful research project. He speaks from considerable experience, having published many research reports in a variety of respected research journals.

The next two chapters address publishing articles in practitioner-oriented journals. Jensen provides suggestions on writing for journals whose audience consists primarily of school-based personnel. She writes from an editor's perspective, since she served as editor of NCTE's elementary journal, *Language Arts*, for 7 years. Baumann describes in detail a procedure he has found useful in preparing manuscripts for publication in various practitioner journals in our field. Since he has written and published many articles, his perspective primarily is that of an author, although he does provide some editorial insight drawn from his experience as editor of IRA's elementary/preschool journal, *The Reading Teacher*.

The final two chapters of Part 1 involve writing for still other types of periodical publications. Micklos discusses how to prepare news articles, columns, and features for publication in literacy newspapers or newsletters. As editor of IRA's newspaper, *Reading Today*, he specifically addresses this outlet, although his suggestions apply equally to those interested in writing for other education newspapers or for the various newsletters published by IRA affiliates. Hopkins provides information about writing reviews of professional and instructional materials for possible publication in literacy periodicals. While acknowledging that there are a variety of approaches to review writing, she presents a clear and direct set of suggestions for how one might structure a review.

The first two chapters of Part 2, which deals with publishing materials for children and young adults, address writing trade books for children. Livingston provides a personal view of what it means to write materials for children. She is well qualified to provide this perspective, given her international reputation as a poet, author, anthologist, and educator. Kruse looks at the more pragmatic aspects of writing trade books for children and young adults. Kruse directs the Cooperative Children's Book Center at the University of Wisconsin-Madison, a library that houses one of the world's most complete collections of children's trade books.

The next two chapters provide insight into the process of publishing commercial reading and language arts programs for children. Pikulski describes 10 phases involved in publishing a reading program. As a senior author on several editions of a successful reading program, he is well qualified to describe this process. A different perspective on publishing reading and language arts programs is presented by Orrell. Orrell, an executive editor for a major educational publisher, discusses the roles of various players involved in developing a reading program.

The final two chapters of Part 2 deal with other types of instructional materials. Johnson describes the process of authoring supplemental materials in reading and language arts, drawing from his considerable experience in writing such materials. Radencich provides practical information about conceiving, writing, and publishing educational microcomputer software. She knows this process well, since she has published a successful vocabulary and comprehension computer software program.

The final section of the book provides information about publishing textbooks and professional books. Howard and Canavan provide specifics about publishing these types of books. These authors have guided numerous book manuscripts through the publication process in their various editorial and managerial roles with commercial textbook publishers. Otto, the author of many college textbooks, contributed the book's final chapter. He conveys his view of the process of writing books through the eyes of his alter ego, Fats Grobnik, a humorous character who is chock-full of wisdom on this and other subjects.

We hope you will find something here to inform you, to impassion you, to entertain you, or maybe even to provoke you. Writing is neither easy nor devoid of ego and emotion. (When asked how it felt to write *John Brown's Body*, Steven Vincent Benét aptly replied, "Just about like giving birth to a grand piano.") We must admit, however, that writing is indeed satisfying and rewarding.

> One ought only to write when one leaves a piece of one's own flesh in the inkpot, each time one dips one's pen.
>
> —Leo Tolstoy

JFB
DDJ

Contributors

James F. Baumann
University of Georgia
Athens, Georgia

Susanne F. Canavan
Christopher-Gordon
Publishers, Inc.
Norwood, Massachusetts

Carol J. Hopkins
Purdue University
W. Lafayette, Indiana

Hiram G. Howard
Christopher-Gordon
Publishers, Inc.
Norwood, Massachusetts

Julie M. Jensen
University of Texas at Austin
Austin, Texas

Dale D. Johnson
Instructional Research and
Development Institute
Boston, Massachusetts

Edward J. Kameenui
University of Oregon
Eugene, Oregon

Ginny Moore Kruse
Cooperative Children's Book
Center, University of
Wisconsin-Madison
Madison, Wisconsin

Myra Cohn Livingston
University of California, Los
Angeles
Los Angeles, California

John Micklos, Jr.
International Reading
Association
Newark, Delaware

Cynthia J. Orrell
Silver Burdett & Ginn
Needham Heights,
Massachusetts

Wayne Otto
University of Wisconsin-
Madison
Madison, Wisconsin

John J. Pikulski
University of Delaware
Newark, Delaware

Marguerite C. Radencich
Dade County Public Schools
Miami, Florida

S. Jay Samuels
University of Minnesota
Minneapolis, Minnesota

P A R T ONE

Publishing in
Journals,
Newspapers,
and Newsletters

■ ■ ■ ■

CHAPTER ONE

Publishing Requirements for Research-Oriented Journals

S. Jay Samuels

Publishing in research-oriented journals has been compared to walking across a mine field at night, where a false step can lead to destruction. Skilled soldiers, however, have learned how to cross these dangerous areas in safety. Samuels, a professor of educational psychology and a well-known researcher, explains how to avoid the pitfalls of publishing in research journals and suggests what steps to take to get articles accepted.

■ ■ ■ ■

Each researcher must try to learn from the work of those who preceded him and to add to a unified body of knowledge—knowing that neither he nor anyone following him will ever have the final word.

—Jeanne Chall

As a graduate student contemplating a career as a university professor, I had a host of anxieties. One of these anxieties reflected my concern about my ability to perform adequately on the job. I worried about being able to get my work published in reputable journals if I got a job as a professor at a publish-or-perish institution. With these problems on my mind, I had a disturbing dream one night. I was in a military tank hidden at the edge of a forest, and my goal was to cross an open field to reach the other side. As soon as I began to cross the field, sharpshooters whom I could not see began to fire antitank weapons at me. They fired at every part of my tank in an attempt to locate a major weakness. Unfortunately, I awoke from the dream before I could find out if I reached my destination.

When I analyzed the dream, I realized that it was a thin veil for my anxieties about getting my research published. The hidden sharpshooters who were firing at me were actually editors and editorial advisory board members looking for weaknesses in my research. Most authors who submit articles to research journals feel vulnerable and wonder about how they can improve their chances for getting published.

Now, with the accuracy of 20-20 hindsight, I can look back and realize that although my anxieties had a modicum of truth, getting published in research-oriented journals is not as hard as I had imagined. Many factors, some of them unrelated to the quality of the manuscript itself, influence editorial decisions to publish or to reject a manuscript. By knowing what editors look for in a manuscript and understanding the hidden factors that influence editorial decisions, authors can improve their acceptance rate.

Consequently, in this chapter I offer advice and some guidelines for publishing in research journals such as the *Reading Research Quarterly* (RRQ). As a former coeditor of this journal, an editorial advisor for other research journals, and a contributor to still others, I can offer several perspectives on how to get published. Since the requirements for getting published in RRQ are similar to the requirements for other research journals, what I say about RRQ generalizes to other journals such as the *Journal of Reading Behavior*, the *American Educational Research Journal*, the *Journal of Educational Psychology*, *Research in the Teaching of English*, and the like.

In giving advice to others, I am mindful of the need for caution suggested by a young student who wrote: "Socrates was a very wise man. He gave advice to all the people of Athens. They killed him." Thus, I offer advice realizing that there is danger in doing so.

Before getting into the details about how to write for research-oriented journals, I would like to present an overview of the topics addressed here. The chapter starts out by describing why a writer needs to be familiar with the editorial policies and audience of the journal in which he or she wishes to publish. Journals that contain scientific content usually require that articles conform to a particular text structure; the writer should know what the requirements are before submitting an article. The second section explains what editors and reviewers look for as they evaluate a manuscript for possible publication. Part of this section is devoted to what can be thought of as pitfalls in writing and offers advice on some things to avoid in preparing a manuscript. The final section of the chapter addresses anxieties the writer may have about being treated fairly in the review process and outlines the probability of being published in a research-oriented journal.

Knowing Journal Policies and Guidelines

Which Professional Audience Do I Want to Address?

Large organizations such as the International Reading Association (IRA), the National Council of Teachers of English (NCTE), and the American Educational Research Association (AERA) publish a number of journals as a service to their members and to the teaching profession. For example, IRA publishes four journals: *The Reading Teacher*, the *Journal of Reading*, *Reading Research Quarterly*, and *Lectura y Vida*. Because each fits a different educational niche, it is prudent for authors to know the policies and guidelines of each journal before writing and submitting articles.

IRA's journals are designed to meet the needs of different educational groups; consequently, each one's circulation and writing style are different. *The Reading Teacher* has by far the largest circulation (more than 65,000 subscribers, mostly classroom teachers). RRQ has a much smaller circulation (about 12,000 subscribers, mostly university-based educational researchers). However, if you compare RRQ's circulation with those of similar journals, you will discover that it is one of the most widely read journals in education research.

As an author, if you want to address primarily practicing educators, submit to *The Reading Teacher* (preschool and elementary levels) or the *Journal of Reading* (adolescent and adult levels). If you want to communicate with academic researchers, submit to RRQ. To reach a Spanish-speaking audience, select *Lectura y Vida*. Choose non-IRA journals with the same eye toward audience appropriateness.

What Are the Journal's Requirements for Submitting an Article?

Failure to follow journal policies and guidelines often leads to rejection of an article. While common sense dictates that an author get the latest copy of a journal to find out where and how to submit an article, it seems that common sense is not always common practice. Occasionally an article is sent to the wrong place, or too few copies are submitted, or the article is written for the wrong audience. Before sending an article for review, get the latest copy of the journal and check to see that you have the correct address and the current editor. Be sure to send along the exact number of copies required. Also, while it is not always required, it is a good idea to include a self-addressed stamped envelope or postcard that the editor can use to acknowledge receipt of the manuscript. After receiving such acknowledgment, allow approximately three months for the review. If you do not get a response by then, write to the editor and ask about your paper.

In addition to knowing where and how to submit an article, authors need to be informed about a target journal's focus, editorial policy, recommended article length, and style. Journals often print this information either on an inside cover or on the pages at the beginning or end of the journal. While all IRA journals contain a policy statement, the statements do not contain all the information an author might want. However, each journal has a printed "Instructions for Authors" brochure that provides detailed information about the publication's audience, style, format, requirements for manuscript preparation, and review policy. These brochures can be obtained by writing to either the current journal editor(s) or the Journals Division at IRA headquarters. Most other research journals that publish articles on literacy have similar brochures.

Does the Journal Require a Particular Writing Style?

Authors should study current issues of IRA journals to determine how each one differs from the others in style. Several important differences can be identified immediately. Articles in RRQ resemble those published in other research-oriented journals such as the *Journal of Educational Psychology*; these articles tend to be longer and more formal than those in classroom-oriented journals.

Just as symphonies and fairy tales adhere to well-established forms, so too do most articles published in educational research journals. The standard structure includes: (1) an abstract; (2) a literature review section that includes a statement of the research problem and its importance; (3) a method section that includes information about the study's subjects, procedures, materials, tasks, and research design; (4) a results section where data from the study are presented; (5) a discussion section; and (6) a reference section.

Research journals are geared toward a specific audience that has certain expectations about content and style. For example, RRQ, with its highly structured, almost pedantic style, is intended for college researchers; in contrast, less formal journals such as *The Reading Teacher* are aimed at classroom teachers. In general, it would be fair to say that articles in research journals present considerably more quantitative and qualitative data than do journals intended for classroom teachers. Thus, longer articles (beyond approximately 15 doublespaced, typewritten pages) with an intended academic research audience should be sent to research journals such as RRQ.

In terms of style, many research journals (including RRQ) have the same requirements as those found in the *Publication Manual of the American Psychological Association* (1983). Some journals may have different style requirements, however. For example, whereas the "Teaching, Learning, and Human Development" section of the *American Educational Research Journal* uses APA style, the *Chicago Manual of Style* (1982) is preferred for the same journal's "Social and Institutional Analysis" section.

Having research articles conform to well-recognized structural and style requirements, whatever the specifics may be, is an excellent practice because when the text matches the reader's expectations, it facilitates text comprehension and recall (Samuels et al., 1988). Adhering to the correct guidelines for a given journal will help authors seeking publication because it is seen as helping readers.

What Editors Look for in a Manuscript

Is the Writing Comprehensible?

Critiquing a manuscript is a difficult, time-consuming, stressful task. The reviewer, mindful of how much effort the author has put into writing the manuscript, wants to see the manuscript get published. At the same time, he or she is a gatekeeper who must recommend for publication only those manuscripts that meet the criteria of good research.

Because of the difficulty of the task, reviewers or editorial advisory board members hope the articles they read will be comprehensible. In a discipline so concerned with reading comprehension and good writing, it is surprising how often one encounters articles that are poorly written and difficult to understand. I have often suspected that authors with little to say have tried to hide this fact behind a cloak of obscure writing. While complex ideas often require complex sentences, it is the writer's responsibility to try to state the complex in as simple and comprehensible a way as possible.

Is the Research Topic Significant?

Beyond the most basic requirement that manuscripts be easy to comprehend, the manuscript reviewer looks for articles that address important issues. Whereas inferential statistics can indicate when two treatment means differ significantly, no statistics can reveal whether a given research topic is significant. The ability to determine whether a scientific study addresses a significant topic comes only with years of experience and extensive knowledge of the subject matter. Judging the significance of a topic is as highly developed an art as knowing whether a chess move is a good one.

At times, editorial board members receive articles that display excellent methodology and writing but that address old research problems no longer considered important; or reviewers may get manuscripts in which the problem addressed, though timely, is trivial. If the reviewers believe an article discusses an outdated or trivial topic, they will usually recommend rejection. Just because the author believes the topic is important is no reason to expect that others will share this belief.

In order to protect against the possibility that a reviewer will not appreciate a manuscript's significance, it is usually wise for an author to explain early in the paper why the research addresses an important issue. In fact, I have noticed that in public lectures, even well-known professors devote a considerable portion of their introduction to convincing the audience that the topic is important.

Is the Study Well Designed?

Beyond the need for comprehensibility and a research topic of significance, still other requirements must be considered before a manuscript can be accepted for publication. Reviewers will examine the logic of an investigation to decide if the method and design of the study are appropriate. Research can be conducted using an experimental/quantitative, ethnographic/qualitative, historical, philosophical, or case study method, among others. In all cases, the method employed must match the question under investigation.

For example, assume that a researcher wanted to test the hypothesis that children with reading problems could learn to read more easily if they used a nonalphabetic symbol system such as Chinese. In this type of system, symbols map directly onto meanings. (Examples of symbols that map directly onto meanings include $, +, −, and =.)

To test the hypothesis, the researcher takes a sample of learning-disabled students and randomly assigns half of them to an experimental condition and the other half to a control condition. The task for both groups is to learn to read 10 words using a look-say (sight word, nondecoding) method. The experimental group is given 10 words written in Chinese orthography, while the control group is given the same 10 words written in English orthography. Once both groups are done, data analysis indicates that the experimental group learned the words in significantly fewer trials than the control group. The researcher concludes that learning-disabled students should learn to read using Chinese symbols. Should this study be published?

Although at a superficial level this study seems satisfactory, a closer look reveals a serious flaw in the logic of the design. To be considered a skilled reader, one must be able to recognize thousands of words rapidly and automatically. Ten words is not a sufficiently large sample to test the hypothesis. What would happen if students had to learn hundreds of words?

Since learning to read in a nonalphabetic language places a heavy load on memory, it is probable that the initial advantage in learning 10 words would be lost when the list was expanded to hundreds. Chinese researchers report that memory problems are considerable in learning to read with their writing system. Thus, an article on the study just described should be rejected on logical grounds because the method did not provide an adequate test of the hypothesis and, consequently, the conclusions are invalid.

Is the Method Section Detailed Enough to Allow Replication by Others?

In addition to evaluating the significance of the research topic and the logic of the design, reviewers examine the method section to see if enough information is given on subject selection, materials, and procedures. In essence, the reviewers look for enough detail to permit another researcher to replicate the study. For example, a description of the subjects who took part in the study should include information on whether they were selected randomly or by some other method. Reviewers also want to know the subjects' ages, grade levels, reading ability, socioeconomic status, intelligence level, and any other information relevant to understanding the findings.

Often, information that we would like to have about the subjects is unavailable. Many schools lack data on students' IQ levels or socioeconomic status. Researchers must then decide whether to omit this information or gather it on their own. In general, researchers should collect and include in the research report all relevant information about the subjects.

Reviewers will also look for a precise description of the materials and procedures used in the study. For example, the author should fully describe any reading materials used. Were the materials narrative or expository? How long were they? What were their readability levels? What topics did the selections cover? Descriptions of procedures also should be thorough, with sufficient detail to permit other researchers to replicate the study.

How Are the Results Reported?

Editorial advisory board members also examine manuscripts to be sure the author has reported and analyzed the data properly. Every reader of a research study wants an overall picture of the investigation's findings. In addition, the data analysis must match the research methods. Transcripts of protocols or rich verbal descriptions may be appropriate for qualitative or ethnographic methods, but experimental/quantitative methods require means, standard deviations, and inferential statistics. I strongly recommend that authors examine recent copies of well-regarded research journals to see the variety of techniques other researchers have used to present their findings.

Are the Results Reliable?

Reviewers look for two additional features in a study: generalizability and replicability. Editors would be very pleased if researchers were able to develop theories so robust that they would hold true across populations, tasks, and materials. We realize, however, that this ideal is seldom, if ever, attainable (Samuels, 1984). Consequently, reviewers and editors instead look for replicability. They want to be convinced that if another scientist were to duplicate the study described in the manuscript under review, similar results would be obtained.

There are a number of ways to convince reviewers and editors that the results are replicable. Assume a researcher wishes to show that a particular type of training leads to better comprehension. The theory is confirmed when, in a careful study, an experimental group significantly outperforms a control group. One way to make such a finding even more convincing is to use two passages instead of one. If the experimental group performs better on both passages, the results are more likely to be reliable. Another way to convince reviewers of a study's reliability is to replicate the study and report both findings in the same article.

Does the Article Meet the Journal's Basic Requirements?

Because the task of reviewing a manuscript is so time consuming and expensive, editors may initially screen all incoming manuscripts to see if they meet the journal's most rudimentary requirements. The initial screening is usually for structure and style. Is the manuscript aimed at the appropriate audience? If it is an experimental report, did the author use the correct structure and reference style? Depending on how severe the departures are from what is required, the editor may decide to send the article back to the author without a full peer review. If the manuscript has only a minor problem, such as failure to list references in the correct style, the paper will usually get a full review. Above all, the editor strives for fairness.

Any of a number of more serious problems, however, will likely cause the manuscript to be returned without review or rejected by the editorial advisory board. The following list outlines common pitfalls that authors would do well to avoid.

- Submitting a manuscript that has spelling errors.
- Sending copy that is unnecessarily difficult to read.
- Failing to doublespace and leave wide margins for editorial comments.
- Submitting the manuscript to the wrong editor.
- Including an incomplete or outdated literature review.
- Failing to let the reader know as soon as possible what question is being studied.
- Inadequately describing the sample, materials, task, design, and procedures.

- Neglecting to include descriptive statistics or to adequately describe the findings using suitable figures, diagrams, transcripts, protocols, or tables.
- Failing to relate the study's findings to research reported in the literature review.
- Failing to use appropriate journal form for citing references.

Fair Treatment in the Review Process

How Are Editors Selected?

Partly because it is important for researchers to communicate with other scholars through articles published in journals and partly because reading is such a controversial topic, the selection of journal editors and the subsequent review and evaluation of their work is viewed as a major endeavor by the parent organization. For example, the International Reading Association initially appoints the editors of RRQ for 4 years; after a review of their work, the editors can be reappointed for an additional 2-year term.

Selecting new journal editors is a time-consuming process. For example, it takes over a year to select RRQ editors. The selection committee looks for an editorial team with members who have solid reputations as reading researchers and who have earned the respect of the academic research and reading communities. The team should also have the ability to get the journal issues out on time. Equally important, the selection committee must have confidence that the editors will be fair to all who wish to publish and not favor articles that support their views. After all, from an ethical stance, the journal represents the views of all of its members, not just those of the current editors.

Once the committee is satisfied that it has appropriate individuals who can satisfy the established criteria, it makes a recommendation to the Association's Board of Directors. After much discussion and analysis of the committee's work, the Board makes the final selection.

How Are Editorial Advisory Board Members Selected?

As a former coeditor of RRQ, I can tell you how concerned everyone was about the problem of fairness. In selecting our editorial advisory board for the journal, we tried to choose persons who represented a variety of views on the reading process. In choosing board members, we kept the following criteria in mind: area of expertise, research paradigm used to investigate problems, instructional approaches to reading, sex, ethnic background, geographic location, international representation, and ability to evaluate research on scientific merit. In all but the last criterion we sought diversity to increase fairness. When the evaluation committee evaluated us after our initial appointment, we had to demonstrate that decisions to publish or reject submitted articles were made on the basis of scientific merit and not for reasons of personal bias.

What Are My Chances of Acceptance?

The editor of any journal faces two major problems. First, when preparing each issue, the editor is faced with empty pages that have to be filled with good material. Depending on the journal—especially if the journal is new—the editor may not have enough good articles to fill the pages. Second, regardless of how prestigious a journal is, it must always compete with other influential journals for good research articles. For example, RRQ competes with *Reading Psychology*, the *Journal of Reading Behavior*, the *Journal of Memory and Language*, *Reading Research and Instruction*, *Child Development*, *Cognitive Psychology*, *Psychological Review*, and the *Journal of Educational Psychology*, among others.

The fact that the editor is faced with empty pages and tough competition is good news for the scholar who wants to get published. There is a great demand for scholarly work, especially when it meets the standards of scientific research. In fact, the demand for articles can become so great that editors may use a variety of techniques to solicit manuscripts. If my dream of graduate school days could get a rerun, it should have journal editors on the fringes of the forest cheering me on through the shelling. After all, they need the articles I have to offer. A rule of thumb is that a good article can always find a home somewhere. All the author needs is perseverance. If one journal does not want your work, try another.

A rule of thumb is. that a good article can always find a home somewhere. ■ ■ ■

To a large extent, the law of supply and demand determines the acceptance rate of a journal. On the supply side are the number of pages a journal has available, the size of type used, the amount of white space in the journal, and the length of the articles published. On the demand side is the number of researchers who want to publish in that journal. Obviously, if the number of articles submitted for publication greatly exceeds the journal's capacity, the journal is likely to have a low acceptance rate. Another possibility, however, is that the journal will have a large backlog of accepted manuscripts; when this happens, an article may have to wait a year or more before being published.

Generally, the older, more prestigious journals have lower acceptance rates and longer in-press waiting periods. The author must decide if it is better to submit an article to one of these journals or to a newer or less prestigious journal that has a higher acceptance rate and a shorter in-press time. Either choice has advantages.

If you receive a letter from an editor that says "publish contingent on proper revision" or "resubmit," consider yourself lucky and revise and resubmit the article as soon as possible. I cannot tell you how often we sent letters to authors asking for a revision and then never heard from them again. When an author revises and resubmits, usually the paper is accepted. In resubmitting an article, enclose a cover letter specifying in what ways the original article was revised. This helps the editor recognize immediately what is different in the new manuscript.

A parting bit of advice: If an article is turned down by a journal, find out why. Usually, a detailed evaluation of the research is given. This evaluation, written by some of the best researchers, contains clues as to how to improve the paper. Revise the manuscript according to those suggestions and submit it elsewhere. With this method, a good piece of research can usually get published. Finally, if you believe that you have received a poor review—this happens on rare occasions—you may wish to explain to the editor the reasons for your dissatisfaction. If your letter is convincing, the editor may have your article reevaluated.

By following the advice I have offered, you should be able to enhance your chances of publishing in a good research journal. I hope my advice has been helpful and that you will spare me the fate of Socrates.

References

Chall, J. (1967). *Learning to read: The great debate*. New York: McGraw-Hill.

The Chicago manual of style (13th ed., rev.). (1982). Chicago: University of Chicago Press.

Publication manual of the American Psychological Association (3rd ed.). (1983). Washington, DC: American Psychological Association.

Samuels, S.J. (1984). Resolving some theoretical and instructional conflicts of the 1980s. *Reading Research Quarterly, 19,* 390-392.

Samuels, S.J., Tennyson, R., Sax, L., Mulcahy, P., & Schermer, N. (1988). Adults' use of text structure in the recall of a scientific journal article. *Journal of Educational Research, 81,* 171-174.

CHAPTER TWO

Guarding Against the False and Fashionable in Research Journals

Edward J. Kameenui

In this chapter, Kameenui presents insight into the process of conceptualizing and studying an empirical problem that merits publication in a research journal. While the previous chapter discusses how to prepare and submit a manuscript, Kameenui focuses on scientific inquiry and the various dimensions of theory building and development. He emphasizes the need for authors to align the theory underlying their research question with the appropriate methodology to ensure conceptual coherence. Kameenui is a widely published researcher and has served on the editorial advisory boards of several national research journals.

■ ■ ■ ■

My intent in this chapter is to examine the process of inquiry that serves as the foundation for publishing in research journals. Such a purpose is admittedly in contrast to specifying the step-by-step practical considerations for getting published. However, I would argue that if the purpose behind getting published is not considered seriously and thoughtfully, having a paper published will be the equivalent of the tail wagging the dog. My observations in this chapter are predicated on the assumption that if the process of inquiry is thoughtful, passionate, well-planned, and anchored in a reasoned way of looking at the world, the results of the inquiry will indeed be published.

In an essay more than 30 years ago, Jacob Bronowski, a mathematician and a man of letters, drew distinctions between the processes of discovery, invention, and creation:

> There are contexts in which one of these words is more appropriate than the others. Christopher Columbus discovered the West Indies, and Alexander Bell invented the telephone. We do not call their achievements creations because they are not personal enough.... By contrast, we feel that *Othello* is genuinely a creation. This is not because *Othello* came out of a clear sky; it did not. There were Elizabethan dramatists before Shakespeare.... Yet within their tradition *Othello* remains profoundly personal; and though every element in the play has been a theme of other poets, we know that the amalgam of these elements is Shakespeare's; we feel the presence of his single mind (cited in Gingerich, 1986, p. 3).

And what of science and the process of experimentation? Is the process of scientific inquiry and experimentation akin to invention, creation, or discovery? If I read Bronowski's essay correctly, scientific inquiry involves all of these things. The real charm and magic of science rests in the hands of the experimenter who starts with a cup of known facts, adds a dash of discovery, and with deliberate strokes stirs the concoction to keep time with the temporal murmurings of the theoretical winds. Finally, the creation is left to brood for two nights under a lucky star. When it's cooled and the time for seeing and tasting is at hand—oh, what results, what magic, what disappointment, what discovery!

What does all this fluff about creation, invention, discovery, and scientific experimentation have to do with writing for research journals? Or more directly, what does it have to do with getting published in research journals? My response is everything—and nothing.

Everything, because publishing does not end with the acceptance of a manuscript for publication, nor does it begin with the writing of a manuscript explicitly for publication. It begins with a personal passion for discovery, creation, invention, and experimentation: a passion for seeing something new or seeing something old in a new light. Or as Nobel-winning physicist Arthur Schawlow notes, the process often begins with "a looking for gaps" (1982, p. 41). The process ends when the passion for discovery, creation, and invention ends.

Discovery, creation, invention, and experimentation can become meaningless when too much emphasis is placed on publishing. Publishing is easily reduced to a recipe of knowledge—a kind of dot-to-dot process in which one's behavior is calibrated with just the right amount of intention and deliberation to bring about just the right product or result. This focus makes more of the product—namely the publication—than it really is, while stripping the process of its charm and spirit.

I remember too clearly telling an English professor and poet friend that I was going to pursue a doctorate in education instead of what he considered to be my calling in English literature. I remember his silence and his cold, direct stare. After a long pause, he said, "Ed, be careful. There is much that is false and fashionable in that." The potential for research to be false and fashionable is especially great if the aim of getting published begins to drive the process of inquiry.

When it comes to publishing, research writers are primarily concerned with the procedural requirements of getting published in research journals, which ostensibly is one focus of this chapter. But you can already sense my schizophrenia about such a focus. It seems cryptic, uninteresting, and myopic to talk about publishing without also talking about why publishing is important and what the final product—a printed article disseminated for public scrutiny—really represents. Too often, we fail to discern with much care what a publication ultimately does or should represent.

In keeping with my schizophrenia, I have decided to give equal time to both personalities. First I will examine the right brain aspect of publishing research—the creation, invention, discovery, and experimentation that lead up to the preparation of a manuscript. Then I will examine the left brain aspect—the procedural tasks of writing, rewriting, submitting, and resubmitting a manuscript for publication. Throughout these discussions, I have attempted to frame and anchor my comments around a set of one-word descriptors to illustrate my main points.

Obviously, conducting research and preparing it for publication is not a dichotomous endeavor. It requires a wholeness of purpose and resources. However, by examining the two sets of requirements separately, we gain a greater appreciation for the process of inquiry and publishing as a whole.

Invention, Creation, and Discovery in Educational Experimentation

Scientific inquiry involves creation, invention, experimentation, and, of course, discovery. Such a process is rarely devoid of form, function, or foils. However, the potential for it to be concerned only with form and function is real. As researchers we have a special responsibility to the process of inquiry, not merely to its form and function.

Community

As practitioners and researchers we are—by design, default, or serendipity—members of a larger educational, scientific, and artistic community. Our actions as individual researchers always affect the larger community. Membership in that group affords us certain privileges. For example, it allows us to work with the most precious commodity there is—children.

But membership also bestows upon us numerous obligations, and debate about the nature of those obligations is endless. I would argue that our primary responsibility is the search for truth, which neither ends with the discovery of statistically significant results nor is automatically fulfilled and sanctified by years of bylines in prestigious professional journals. That search, although profoundly personal, is always nested in a broader, collective context. A statistically significant finding or discovery does not in and of itself represent truth; it acquires meaning and truth only when fellow researchers are allowed to touch, stretch,

Scientific inquiry involves creation, invention, experimentation, and, of course, discovery. ■ ■ ■

question, and replicate its genuineness. Descartes observed that "Truths are more likely to have been discovered by one man than by a nation." However, as individual researchers seeking the truth, we know that truths are sustained not by one man or woman but by a community of men and women.

As a researcher, it is important to seek membership in professional communities early in one's career. Examples of professional organizations include the International Reading Association, the National Reading Conference, the American Educational Research Association, the Association for Supervision and Curriculum Development, and the Council for Exceptional Children. Membership in this type of organization allows a beginning researcher to gain a sense of the scholarship and values held by a community of professionals.

Dubitation

Membership in this professional community obligates us to engage in a questioning process, not merely to deliver a product that reports statistically significant differences (Kerlinger, 1977). The value of the product of this process, the published manuscript, is always less than that of the process itself. I call this questioning process *dubitation*, a term borrowed from a former English professor who taught me to appreciate Hamlet's often-quoted fourth soliloquy. (In the past, I have confessed to doctoral students that I've learned more about the process of inquiry by reading and rereading Shakespeare than I have from all my studies of the social, behavioral, and psychological sciences.)

Scientific or artistic inquiry is the process of posing a doubt, not unlike Hamlet's query, "To be or not to be." But posing the doubt is not enough. The researcher must walk the doubt through until it is clarified, solved, or seen *de novo*—with fresh eyes. This process was captured best by an article in *Ms. Magazine* brought to my attention by a student. In that article, Gornick (1983) discusses the moment when Laura Levin, a 51-year-old biophysicist, suddenly saw something new. Levin had been working for years on the molecular structure of the special muscle mechanism that keeps the clam from being easily pried open (a problem, believe it or not, that scientists have worked on since the turn of the century). Levin describes that moment:

> I felt I was born for that moment. To stand there, on that street in Paris in the middle of the night, with this idea at last clarified in my mind. Oh, that clarification! It was as though the idea had come into my head so that one day I would know the incredible joy of that clarification. Nothing else can touch that experience for me. Let me tell you, there's not an "I love you" in the world that can touch it. Nothing (p. 52).

Oh, what magic, what discovery, what dubitation!

You can get that same sense of unbridled spirit and joy in clarification in *The Double Helix* by Nobel laureate James Watson (1968), who, with Francis Crick, discovered the structure of DNA. So the concern for publishing in professional journals should be born out of an intense desire to seek the truth, not an intense desire merely to publish the truth. It is in the seeking and clarifying, not the publishing, that we best meet the obligations of our membership in the larger scientific and artistic community.

Connoisseurship

I have borrowed this descriptor from Eisner (1977), who has written extensively on educational connoisseurship and criticism. The search for truth requires a passion for seeking, probing, puzzling, brooding, and knowing. This connoisseurship (from the Latin word *cognoscere*, "to know") is fed by what Snow (1973) refers to as a *zeitgeist*, "the source of the puzzles that motivate the scientist to theorize, the metaphors that inspire that theorizing, and the mental habits that shape the result" (p. 79).

Connoisseurship does not express itself only within a scientific paradigm. Instead, it is an "appreciative art" in which the artist (or scientist) has a keen awareness of the characteristics and qualities of whatever he or she encounters (Eisner, 1977, p. 2). This connoisseurship must also be balanced by criticism, or what Eisner calls the "art of disclosure," in which the critic provides a rendering of what it is he or she has encountered so others may encounter it in their own way (p. 3).

To summarize the right brain aspect of this discussion, publications should represent the final product of a process in which the writer/researcher acknowledges the connection to a larger community, is immersed in knowledge about something (i.e., connoisseurship), and engages in inquiry (i.e., dubitation) and a search for truth.

Those who seek practical guidance for getting published will note that my advice so far offers little about the business of publishing. My only defense for this impractical advice is that community, connoisseurship, and the process of dubitation have everything to do with the practice of science, the development of theory, and the establishment of a sustained program of inquiry that should result in the publication and dissemination of tested observations. In the absence of this passion for inquiry or discovery, getting published is likely to be a fragmented and meaningless exercise.

Procedural Knowledge of Publishing

Now for the left brain—the dry, logical, and procedural part of publishing. In my limited literature search, I was surprised by several articles on what is referred to as the "publication game." The existence of the articles didn't surprise me, but their thoughtfulness and apparently valid content did. I have borrowed much from one article to help me organize this part of my chapter. Interestingly, the author of this article chose to remain unnamed (Anonymous, 1987).

Silk

My first descriptor for this part of the brain is silk. Our efforts to delineate the rules of publishing suggest that the rules are stated, agreed upon, and well known. They are not. Journals will provide you with guidelines for packaging a manuscript. However, the rules for describing how to fit the contents into this package are not clear. The journals present only positive examples of how to get published. As we know, it is difficult, if not impossible, to learn a concept by examining only positive examples (Jitendra & Kameenui, 1988). Negative examples depicting how not to get published also are critical. In fact, it may be easier to talk about how not to get published than how to get published.

It's fair to say that if a research study is methodologically flawed, theoretically insignificant, and programmatically unconnected to a larger body of inquiry, its chances of getting published are small (notice I said small, not zero). As the saying goes, you can't turn a sow's ear into a silk purse. The best advice for getting published is simply to conduct methodologically sound, theoretically significant, and programmatically cohesive research. Spin silk and you'll never be caught whispering into a sow's ear again.

Ripeness

I have borrowed this word from Shakespeare's *King Lear* because I think it captures an elusive feature of publishing. By ripeness, I mean "the state or quality of being mature, developed, complete"—a kind of readiness. This ripeness requires a keen and full taste for what is being researched in one's field. As Schawlow (1982) states, "What you hope to develop through experience is scientific taste, some feelings for what's worth doing, and what's possible to do" (p. 39). This ripeness or scientific taste also requires sensitivity and insight into sustained trends and an anticipation of the next step, the next set of issues.

Not surprisingly, such ripeness comes from connoisseurship. I encourage you to keep abreast of research summaries, journal editorials, and other persuasive articles published for the purpose of summarizing findings in an area, in addition to articles that report results of experiments. Professional conferences are also important forums for discerning state-of-the-art issues.

Alignment

A submission to a research journal assumes that you have something new to share with the scientific or artistic community. The successful sharing or publishing of that information requires a careful alignment between your results and the journal you select to make those results public.

To make that external alignment as true as possible, it is important to know the primary research journals in your field. There is simply no substitute for journal reading. This practice allows you to develop an instinct for the editorial idiosyncrasies of particular journals—their preferences in content, style, and format.

Another form of alignment is the internal correspondence of the study's hypotheses and results with a conceptual or theoretical model. The conceptual or theoretical basis of a study's descriptive and operational features is critical to its acceptance for publication.

Persistence

My experience is that if a study is theoretically and methodologically sound (I should add that it doesn't have to be flawless), and the writer is sufficiently persistent, the manuscript will eventually find a home in a journal. This persistence requires developing a thick skin for rejection; it also requires that the writer/ researcher view the process of review as an informative one. Reviews provide the researcher with information about what to do next time in designing a study, as well as how to revise the manuscript to make it acceptable for publication.

My practice is to submit a research paper to the best journal in a given field to obtain the best review and feedback about a piece of work. By incorporating the feedback into my revision, I greatly increase the chances of having the paper accepted, whether in the same journal or another one. Careful revision usually pays off.

Clarity and Specificity

These descriptors refer to the basic standards of sound writing. There is really no excuse for not carefully proofreading your work to detect typos, omissions, and poor typeface choice or quality. Reviewers will tolerate a few of these stylistic errors, but too many of them are annoying and sometimes insulting to the reviewer and the journal.

In the foreword to Bloom's (1987) *The Closing of the American Mind*, Saul Bellow states that "A piece of writing is an offering. You bring it to the altar and hope it will be accepted" (p. 15). A manuscript submitted for publication is often a very personal offering, because the writer seeks acceptance of his or her ideas, interpretations, and insights. A frequent barrier to the acceptance of a manuscript for publication is unclear writing. Wordy, disorganized, or unfocused manuscripts that rely heavily on jargon are likely to be rejected. As a general rule, it's important to tell one story with one voice; the offering should be kept simple.

Supreme Tension

In the last paragraph of the last page of *The Rebel*, Camus (1956) draws an analogy between the nature of rebellion and an archer drawing an arrow to a bow:

> At this moment, when each of us must fit an arrow to his bow and enter the lists anew, to reconquer, within history and in spite of it, that which he owns already, the thin yield of his fields, the brief love of this earth, at this moment...the bow bends, the wood complains. At this moment of supreme tension, there will leap into flight an unswerving arrow, a shaft that is inflexible and free (p. 306).

You may recognize this as a right brain descriptor that somehow got synapsed into the left hemisphere, a phenomenon known as the right hemispherical dominance syndrome. I am told that no amount of medication can correct it. The truth is, I just wanted to end on the right foot.

As writers/researchers, we must take aim at a specific target and persist. We must also align our methodological tools to our theoretical bows. When the target is clear and the alignment true and specific, we will hear the words complain, and our ideas will bend. And at the right moment—that ripe moment of supreme theoretical, pedagogical, and conceptual tension—our ideas will leap into flight, "an unswerving arrow, a shaft that is inflexible and free." There is nothing false and fashionable in that.

References

Anonymous (1987). The publication game: Beyond quality in the search for a lengthy vita. *Journal of Social Behavior and Personality, 2,* 3-12.

Bloom, A. (1987). *The closing of the American mind.* New York: Simon & Schuster.

Camus, A. (1956). *The rebel.* New York: Random House.

Eisner, E. (1977). On the uses of educational connoisseurship and criticism for evaluating classroom life. *Teachers College Record, 78,* 1-14.

Gingerich, O. (1986). *Specific genius and creativity.* New York: W.H. Freeman.

Gornick, V. (1983, October). That moment when you suddenly see something in the world is like nothing else. *Ms. Magazine, 51-52,* 130-135.

Jitendra, A., & Kameenui, E.J. (1988). A design-of-instruction analysis of concept teaching in five basal language programs: Violations from the bottom up. *Journal of Special Education, 22*(2), 199-219.

Kerlinger, F. (1977). The influence of research on education practice. *Educational Researcher, 6,* 5-12.

Schawlow, A. (1982, Fall). Going for the gaps. *Stanford Magazine,* 38-42.

Snow. R. (1973). Theory construction for research on teaching. In R.M.W. Travers (Ed.), *Second handbook of research on teaching: A project of the American Educational Research Association* (pp. 77-112). Chicago, IL: Rand McNally.

Watson, J. (1968). *The double helix: A personal account of the discovery of the structure of* DNA. New York: New American Library.

Kameenui

Reading with a Writer's Eye: Publishing in Practitioner Journals

Julie M. Jensen

In this chapter, Jensen offers advice to authors who wish to enhance their chances of submitting an acceptable manuscript to practitioner journals in the language arts. She emphasizes the importance of reading recent issues of the journal chosen for submission. Doing so, she argues, enables authors to better understand and appreciate its tone, style, and format. She relates her suggestions specifically to her past experience as editor of Language Arts, *elementary journal of the National Council of Teachers of English.*

■ ■ ■ ■

File drawers overflowing with yellowing letters and new letters arriving regularly are a continuing reminder of my 7-year editorship of *Language Arts*—a tenure that ended in 1983:

Julie M. Jensen
406 Education Building
University of Texas
Austin, TX 78712

Dear Dr. Jensen:

I am interested in writing an article for *Language Arts*. How long should it be? Would you like me to send an outline first to see if you are interested? Do you have guidelines for contributors that could be sent to me?...

Language Arts
National Council of Teachers of English
1111 Kenyon Road
Urbana, IL 61801

Dear Sir:

I have written a two-page review of *The Garden of Abdul Gasazi* by Chris Van Allsburg. Would you like to see it?...

Rodney Smith
Editor, *Elementary English*
Florida State Department of Education
Tallahassee, FL 32301

Dear Mr. Smith:

My third graders are writing limericks. Does your journal publish children's writing? How much will they get paid?...

And still more questions sent by potential authors:

- Are you interested in articles about the middle school?
- Do you print letters to the editor?
- May I include photos with my article?
- May I send you a review of the new Ginn language arts program?
- Should I doublespace even my reference list?
- Is it okay that my paper is already in APA style?
- Is the journal refereed?
- How much longer will it take you to make a decision on my manuscript?
- Should I type my name at the top of every page?

- Will you publish this announcement about a conference we're holding next month?
- May I submit my manuscript to more than one journal at a time?
- How many copies of my manuscript do you need?
- Will I get my manuscript back?
- Am I going to receive the page proofs for correction?
- Do I get paid for my article?

These letters are evidence of the multitude of questions and problems faced by would-be writers for publication. They also highlight the writers' lack of basic knowledge about how to submit a manuscript, what types of material are acceptable, and even where to send submissions.

All these letters represent wasted motions and delays for their writers and busywork for an editor. None helped to make *Language Arts* a better journal. With rare exceptions, each was the result of the writer's neglect to heed an obvious, rudimentary, and often repeated bit of advice: Know thy journal.

Picture yourself with a head full of ideas and a heart full of desire to share them. Your topic is one you are thoroughly familiar with and have thought about deeply. It is one you can address with vigor, conviction, and authority. Imagine that you have the skills to write simple, direct prose that says exactly what you want it to say in the fewest words possible. Assume, too, that for one reason or another you have selected *Language Arts* for your manuscript. In doing so, you have, by some rational process, ruled out dozens of alternatives:

- You have chosen a publication with a national instead of a local, regional, state, or international distribution.
- You have chosen a publication with a broad and comprehensive scope, instead of one with a focus on a single aspect of the language arts.

- You have chosen elementary teachers as the most appropriate primary audience for your message, rather than children (reached through *Cricket Magazine*, for example), secondary teachers (*English Journal*), teacher educators (*English Education*), administrators (*National Elementary Principal*), researchers (*Research in the Teaching of English*), or parents and the public (*Family Circle*).
- You have chosen a journal over a newsletter, pamphlet, teacher's guide, workbook, textbook, software program, videotape, or film.
- You have chosen as a sponsor a nonprofit professional organization rather than a commercial press, an education agency, a community group, or a governmental agency.

Reading with the Eyes of a Writer

Although writing and publishing an article involves skill, art, and sometimes politics, and although success lies in practice, perseverance, and careful preparation, this chapter is concerned with only one step in the careful preparation of a manuscript. It offers but one suggestion for increasing the likelihood of acceptance by an editor. While you may be a seasoned reader of *Language Arts*, you may never have read the journal through the eyes of a writer. Of the countless ways I have watched potential authors create obstacles to their success, most common is the failure to locate several *recent* issues and to read them like a writer. From reading like a writer you will learn lessons about substance, form, timing, and procedures that are immediately applicable as you prepare your own manuscript.

With the issues spread before you, take time to make observations about such characteristics as tone, style, philosophical bias, length, preferred kinds of titles, and the role of graphics. Look for features of particular interest to writers. For example, an issue may include calls for manuscripts for other publications as well as for *Language Arts*. Such calls, which typically state preferred topics and deadlines, provide you with critical information about content and timing, as the following example illustrates:

Call for Manuscripts for *Language Arts**

Manuscript Deadline**	Journal Issue	Journal Theme
April 1	September	Children, language, and schools: Making them compatible
May 1	October	Writing: How can teachers best serve young writers?
June 1	November/ December	Teaching reading: What are we proud of?
August 1	January	*Language Arts* at sixty: A retrospective
September 1	February	Oral language: Does anybody care? Then what?
October 1	March	Arts: Self-expression through language
November 1	April	Literature: Research and issues in response to literature; components of a literature-rich school environment
December 1	May	Potpourri: An editor's farewell

*Varied manuscript formats are welcomed. Possibilities include: debates, interviews, point-counterpoint, original poetry, photo essays, position papers, satires, reviews, letters, and program descriptions.

**Earlier manuscript deadlines and themes may be found in *Language Arts*, September 1980, p. 596.

From *Language Arts*, September 1981, p. 632. Reprinted by permission of the National Council of Teachers of English.

From your perusal of the call, you will note that, unlike most journals, all these issues of *Language Arts* had a special theme. Good timing is especially crucial when submitting to a themed journal. If your manuscript arrives by the published deadline, it will likely be processed according to a predictable schedule. If you miss the deadline, publication will be delayed until another topically appropriate issue is scheduled.

As you continue browsing through recent issues, look for commentaries by the editor. Such commentaries can be a window not only on the needs of the journal but on the editor's values in selecting manuscripts. For example, during recent years, every issue of *Language Arts* has begun with a feature called "Dear Readers." During my editorship I used this feature to introduce readers to the articles that followed. I often commented on the general "state of the theme" for that month (e.g., the teaching of listening), sometimes taking my cues from the manuscript pool available to me in putting together the issue. In doing so, I embedded lessons for would-be contributors, as shown in the following excerpt:

Dear Readers:

As an elementary school child, a college student of children's literature, an elementary classroom teacher, a university professor, and an editor of this journal, I have acquired and retained a series of related puzzlements about the teaching of reading—the subject of this issue.

- Why must reading instruction be so technical, complex, competitive, formal, mystical, humorless, tedious, and frustrating?

- In this cliché-infested area of the curriculum, how can so many educators correctly recite or nod agreement with statements like "Children learn to read by reading," and "We want children who not only *can* read, but who *do* read," yet reveal no evidence of having internalized their meaning in classroom practice?

- Though reading *skills* are necessary, why have they become an obsession? (Are skills ends in themselves, or are they means to reading goals?)

I finally became convinced of the value, joy, and potential of children's literature as a college student. Feeling unhappy with that necessary confession, I knew that my role as a classroom teacher involved establishing an environment which helped children to recognize that reading is not an academic pursuit, but a useful and enjoyable way to spend their time. I knew that I had to be a reader, because my role was central in making sure that children got together with the right books. I knew, finally, that whoever the child, whatever the level, program, or method, reading instruction couldn't occur without good literature.

These personal observations close with an editor who, upon examining the largest single component of her manuscript file, continues to wish for more "reading" manuscripts which demystify, which could ultimately help readers to achieve outcomes broader than skills, which show a better balance of concern between teaching for skill and valuing/enjoying, and which call for a climate in society which would allow educators to take as much pleasure in a child who enjoys reading as in one who can get a high test score.

Clearly, many people feel discomfort in the deficiencies of current knowledge and practice. This month's authors have written about both.

From *Language Arts*, February 1977, p. 113. Reprinted by permission of the National Council of Teachers of English.

The message to you as a writer is unmistakable. This editorial (1) alerts you that competition for space in an issue with reading as its theme is stiff since more people think they have something to say about reading than about any other topic; (2) tells you that the editor wants to see more manuscripts that demystify reading, deemphasize skills, stress reading pleasure, and integrate reading with other language arts; and (3) makes it clear that the editor is unlikely to publish essays in which theory is divorced from practice. Careful reading of editorial comments is one way to read like a writer because such comments provide important clues about the kinds of manuscripts a journal editor is seeking.

The Key: Author Guidelines

The single most important resource for you to discover from a study of recent issues of *Language Arts* is the author guidelines, meant explicitly for the potential contributor. Although I printed full author guidelines in every issue, some editors print them only occasionally—one more reason why it is important to examine several recent issues. Still other editors do not print them at all, but announce their availability in small print on the masthead. In that instance you will need to request them by mail, using the address provided. To maximize the odds of your manuscript being accepted for publication, you should follow these guidelines *to the letter*.

Careful reading of editorial comments is one way to read like a writer. ■ ■ ■

Remember those yellowing letters in my file? The ones that did the writer, the editor, and the journal no good? My response to every one of them was exactly the same—one that incorporated the advice I have, in a more leisurely fashion, offered you here. I thanked them for considering *Language Arts* for their work, suggested that they carefully examine a few recent issues, and enclosed a photocopy of the contributor's guide appearing in those issues, highlighting on it the answers to their questions.

Here are excerpts from those venerable guidelines, resurrected to persuade you that they, combined with reading a few recent issues like a writer, respond to the questions, problems, and obstacles faced by the letter writers cited at the beginning of this chapter. (In those progressively rarer instances when the guidelines failed, I responded to the writer with a personal letter and promptly edited the guidelines to remove the newly discovered deficiency.)

Manuscripts

Content: *Language Arts* publishes original contributions on all facets of language arts learning and teaching. Its contents are of primary interest to teachers and teacher educators of children in the preschool through middle school years. Viewpoints not only from education but from academic areas which have implications for language arts teaching (e.g., anthropology, linguistics, psychology) are welcome. Varied manuscript formats are possible, including: debates, interviews, point-counterpoint, original poetry, photo essays, position papers, satires, reviews, letters, and program descriptions. Graphics accompanying manuscripts must be camera ready. Readers are encouraged to submit children's writing and any accompanying drawings. Choose exceptional products—no class sets—and include the child's name, age, school, city, and state....

Preparation: All manuscripts must be...double-spaced throughout, with generous margins, and submitted in triplicate to the Editor. No specific manuscript length is prescribed; however, concise presentations with brief, clear, and interest-capturing titles are valued. A consistent form, in accordance with The University of Chicago Press's A *Manual of Style* is stressed. Although the Editor assumes responsibility for prescreening and final disposition of all submissions, manuscripts are read additionally by at least two reviewers. For this reason, each manuscript should include a cover sheet containing the author's name, position, and address. Identifying information should not appear elsewhere on the manuscript in order to ensure an impartial review. The Editor is able to consider completed manuscripts only, and cannot assess the ultimate appropriateness for the journal of proposals or outlines.

Processing: The length of time required for screening and processing manuscripts varies greatly because of the volume of contributions received and the nature of the publication process, which requires an editor to work several months in advance of the appearance of an issue. Upon receipt of a manuscript an acknowledgement is sent. A decision on the disposition of a manuscript can be reached in as little as one month if copy is submitted according to the schedule of themes published in the September issue. The decision may be delayed for up to one year if this schedule is not observed. It is assumed that the manuscripts submitted to *Language Arts* are previously unpublished and are not under simultaneous consideration by any other publication. One copy of each manuscript not accepted for publication can be returned to the author if it is accompanied by a self-addressed envelope to which stamps are clipped. The Editor reserves the right to revise all accepted manuscripts for clarity, excessive length, and offensive (e.g., sexist) language. Page proofs are not returned to authors for their approval. Publication typically occurs three months following acceptance of a manuscript. Upon publication two complimentary copies of the issue are sent to authors. Reprints may be purchased. *Language Arts* does not pay an honorarium for submissions selected for publication. Manuscripts and correspondence regarding editorial matters should be addressed to:....

From *Language Arts* during the editorship of Julie M. Jensen. Reprinted by permission of the National Council of Teachers of English.

Keep Reading

Today, several years into retirement as an editor, I am convinced that my responsibility to the journal will never completely end. Not a week goes by without a query letter or a manuscript for *Language Arts* in my mailbox. My response is to forward the latest arrival to the current editor.

Although I certainly enjoyed being the editor of *Language Arts*, it does writers no good to send manuscripts to me or to any other incorrect address. While I was editor, dozens of manuscripts each year found their roundabout way to my office in Texas after first going to "Dear Sir" at NCTE headquarters in Illinois or to editors who had preceded me by up to a dozen years. These authors, who failed to consult recent issues, penalized themselves by unnecessarily delaying the processing of their manuscripts. So be kind to yourself. Do your homework; read recent issues. Since good journals are always in flux, it is unsafe to make assumptions across time and across editors.

It is similarly unsafe to make assumptions across publications. Editors do not have comparable policies. Your job is to study the policies and procedures of your selected journal. In the process you may decide the journal is not for you after all. Guidelines for contributors, when studied in detail, may drive you to an alternative publication. You may learn answers that do not please you, answers to questions you had never thought to ask: You don't pay me for my article? I don't get to read the page proofs? I can't send my manuscript to several journals at the same time? You want me to sign over the copyright to the National Council of Teachers of English?

Countless facets of the art and science and politics of writing for professional publication are beyond the scope of this chapter. I have written about some of those facets elsewhere (Jensen, 1982, 1985). These and other articles will provide you with one kind of reading about how to become a published author. Besides reading about writing for publication, you can enhance your chances of producing publishable work by reading about writing in general (e.g., Strunk & White, 1979; Trimble, 1975), by reading good writing constantly, and, of course, by reading like a writer. If you read continually in order to write, the only letter you may ever need to send an editor is one that simply announces the arrival of a masterpiece.

References

Jensen, J.M. (1982). Publishing in the elementary language arts. In S. Judy (Ed.), *Publishing in English and English education*. Portsmouth, NH: Boynton/ Cook.

Jensen, J.M. (1985). Communicating research to teachers. *Journal of Reading Behavior, 17*(2), 93-99.

Strunk, W., & White, E.B. (1979). *The elements of style* (3rd ed.). New York: Macmillan.

Trimble, J.R. (1975). *Writing with style: Conversations on the art of writing*. New York: Prentice Hall.

Preparing and Submitting Articles for Practitioner Journals

James F. Baumann

In this chapter, Baumann presents steps an author might take when conceiving of and writing an article to submit to a reading or language arts journal intended for practitioners. Specifically, he provides suggestions about how to generate an idea for an article, identify and refine the problem, select and write for a target journal, obtain presubmission reviews, prepare and submit the article, and revise and resubmit papers either to the same journal or another one. Baumann, a widely published author, writes mainly from that perspective, although he also draws from his experience as editor of The Reading Teacher.

■ ■ ■ ■

Writing is a dog's life, but the only life worth living.

—Gustave Flaubert

The purpose of this chapter is to present suggestions for how a writer might conceive of, prepare, and submit a manuscript for publication in a practitioner journal in literacy education. By *practitioner journal*, I mean a periodical that presents practical information for teachers, supervisors, and administrators who work with students at the preschool through adult levels. Examples of practitioner journals are *The Reading Teacher* and the *Journal of Reading*, the International Reading Association's (IRA) preschool to elementary and secondary to adult journals, respectively. *Language Arts* and the *English Journal* are the complementary elementary and secondary practitioner journals of the National Council of Teachers of English.

Many additional international, national, and state/provincial journals that publish articles directed toward practicing teachers are listed in the *Contributor's Guide to Periodicals in Reading*, which is updated and published annually by IRA. The *Contributor's Guide* includes information about each publication's audience, content, publication process, style, and current editor and address.

What kinds of submissions are generally entertained by editors of practitioner journals? The answer to this question varies from journal to journal, since each periodical has a somewhat different audience and purpose. However, to give you a flavor of the types of articles found in literacy education journals, several possible topics and formats are listed in Figure 1. These possibilities are adapted from information contained in the "Instructions for Authors" brochure we prepared for *The Reading Teacher*. As you can see, a number of different formats are possible, but each must address in some fashion the teaching or learning of literacy abilities. While this list is specific to *The Reading Teacher*, submissions of this nature would be appropriate for a number of other practitioner journals in reading and language arts.

Most practitioner journals in literacy education are peer reviewed (also called juried or refereed). Peer reviewed means that articles are read and evaluated anonymously by two to four members of an editorial advisory board who are experts on the topic addressed. On the basis of the reviewers' recommendations, the editor will decide whether to accept or reject a work for publication. Therefore, in order to get an article accepted in a practitioner journal, you must convince both the editorial advisory board members and the journal editors that your work is worth publishing.

Figure 1
Possible Formats and Topics
for Articles and Reports

Empirically based teaching strategies

Innovative/exemplary school literacy programs (at the classroom, building, district, or state/provincial level)

Applied research reports (in progress or summative)
- small-scale, classroom-based action research studies
- larger, more formal research reports
- reports using an experimental, qualitative, ethnographic, historical, survey, philosophical, or case study methodology
- "teacher as researcher" and collaborative efforts

Essays on timely or controversial issues in literacy education

Syntheses or reviews of applied research or theory in literacy education

---

Adapted from *The Reading Teacher* "Instructions for Authors" brochure.

In this chapter I describe a process I have used to prepare and submit articles to practitioner journals. The components of the process are: (1) generate an idea for an article, (2) identify and refine the problem, (3) select a target journal, (4) write specifically for the target journal, (5) obtain presubmission reviews from colleagues or friends, (6) revise the article and submit it to the target journal, and (7) celebrate or revise and submit again (either to the same journal, if encouraged to do so, or to a different one). To make the discussion more illustrative, I will relate the publication process to an article I coauthored and had published in a practitioner journal several years ago ("The What, Why, How, and When of Comprehension Instruction," Baumann & Schmitt, 1986).

Most of my comments are based on my experience as an author writing articles for practitioner journals. However, some are based on the knowledge I've acquired as editor of IRA's preschool/elementary practitioner journal, *The Reading Teacher*. Since I've been able to view the publication process from both the author's and the editor's perspective, I can offer tips from both points of view.

Generate an Idea

A sensible place to start the writing process is with an idea. Journal editors and editorial advisory board members are looking for papers that present something new or interesting or, at the minimum, papers that present new applications of existing ideas. How can you go about generating a novel or interesting idea? Where might such an idea come from?

One way to come up with ideas is to be a regular reader of professional journals, newsletters, newspapers, and books. Knowing what issues are topical will help you in considering possible ideas for articles and in evaluating how timely and interesting they might be for readers. A person who is not aware of current developments in literacy education is not likely to generate novel and interesting ideas in this field. Also, reading the work of others may prompt you to think of a related idea.

Besides wide reading, ideas may be derived from a number of sources. Perhaps you have devised an interesting teaching procedure about which you could write. Perhaps a recent university course or workshop has spurred an idea. Look at any paper you have written for graduate reading or language arts courses. Some of my first articles were modified versions of term papers. If you have made a presentation at a local, state/provincial, or national meeting, you may well have the nucleus for an article; the criteria for accepting conference presentations are similar to those used to accept articles for publication. Finally, if you have a paper that you previously submitted to one or more journals but that was never accepted, don't give up on it. More than once I have dusted off an old rejected manuscript, updated it, and ultimately had it accepted for publication.

Where did Maribeth Schmitt and I get the idea for "The What, Why, How, and When of Comprehension Instruction" (WWHW) article? Part of the impetus for writing the article was research I had conducted on reading comprehension instruction (Baumann, 1984, 1986). We decided that an earlier instructional model (Baumann, 1983) did not help students sufficiently to evaluate the effectiveness of a comprehension strategy; nor did it help them with corrective or fix-up strategies. Since Maribeth was working on her dissertation on the related topic of meta-comprehension training, we decided to collaborate on two articles: one being the WWHW article, for which I took the lead author's role, and an article on teaching comprehension monitoring during basal reading instruction, for which she took the lead author's role (Schmitt & Baumann, 1986). Thus, a combination of prior research and writing and current interests prompted us to write these articles.

By the way, working with a coauthor can be helpful in several ways. Obviously, the amount of writing can be reduced if two persons collaborate. But perhaps the greatest benefit to having a coauthor is that you can read, respond to, and edit one another's writing, which helps polish a piece and is likely to enhance your chances of getting a paper accepted. One caveat is in order regarding coauthorship, however: Select your coauthors carefully. You will be working very closely with them, so make certain you are compatible and they are reliable and willing to share the workload. Collaboration can be very helpful, but without the right mix of personalities, you might be better off writing alone.

Identify and Refine the Problem

After generating the idea, you will have to do some research to identify and refine the problem you want to address. This logically involves reading related empirical, theoretical, and applied works in journals, reports, and books. In other words, you will need to use your research skills to identify relevant literature. Sources such as the *Education Index*, the ERIC system, and IRA's *Annual Summary of Investigations Relating to Reading* (Weintraub, annually) will be invaluable for identifying related literature.

Through your research you may find that the seemingly novel idea you generated quite independently has already been addressed in the literature. This may be disappointing, but at least you will save yourself the frustration of writing a paper that duplicates existing material. On occasion we at *The Reading Teacher* have had to reject articles that were interesting and well written but that essentially restated already-published works. In these situations, it was apparent to us that authors had not done their homework since they were unaware of existing articles on their topic. In other situations, authors have failed to acknowledge important research and theory published on a related topic, another indication of failure to do the necessary research.

The research process should enable you to articulate a problem and develop a rationale for writing your article. You may have begun your quest for publication simply with what you consider to be an interesting idea, and that is a fine start, but a good article presents a logical argument or thesis. An author must convince the editors and reviewers that she or he is addressing a new topic or is presenting new ideas about an existing topic if the paper is to be accepted for publication.

Most practitioner journals require a theoretical or empirical basis for the works they publish. This means that authors must present convincing arguments that their contributions extend current knowledge. One format I have found helpful in organizing my thoughts before I begin drafting a piece consists of the following parts:

- *Argument Articulation*. This is a straightforward, logical presentation of what is known and not known about the topic under consideration. An internal structure that has worked well for me when expressing an argument consists of two major components: "We know that..." and "However,..." statements.

We know that...: These are statements about the state of the art of the reading/language arts topic you will address. They form a concise review of relevant published research, theory, or practical information on your topic.

However,...: These are expressions of what knowledge is still lacking—what is *not* known about your topic, either because of limited or nonexistent research or because no one has applied or extended extant knowledge.

- *Statement of Purpose.* Given the "however" information, this is an explicit statement of why you are writing the article and what you intend to accomplish, that is, the rationale or argument for writing the piece. An extension of this component might be a preview of the article's organization.

To illustrate how this structure can help an author articulate an argument and purpose statement, consider the following excerpts from the introduction of the WWHW article:

- *Argument Articulation*

  We know that: "The direct instruction of reading comprehension has been discussed with increasing frequency in the research literature."

  We know that: "The argument has essentially been that when teachers are actively, intensively, and systematically involved with instruction in reading comprehension, students learn to comprehend."

  We know that: "Experimental studies have confirmed this hypothesis by demonstrating that students at various grade levels can be taught effectively a variety of reading skills according to several direct instruction approaches."

However: "Winograd and Hare (in press) reviewed several of these direct instruction studies...to determine if the instruction in these studies included three types of knowledge: declarative, procedural, and conditional."

However: "Comprehension instruction has more often been successful in providing readers with declarative and procedural knowledge (the what and how of comprehension) than it has been in providing the conditional knowledge (the why and when of comprehension) needed to monitor and regulate the use of comprehension skills."

- *Statement of Purpose*: "This article presents a direct instruction approach to reading comprehension that includes all three forms of knowledge. First, each step is described. Next, a sample lesson demonstrates the application of this approach for teaching a traditional reading comprehension skill. The article concludes with a discussion of how reading comprehension skill instruction in commercial materials might be adapted or modified to include all three forms of knowledge."

As these excerpts indicate, this structure can also serve as an outline for the introduction of an article. Sometimes I have worked in this fashion, stating each of the "argument articulation" and "statement of purpose" points in one or two sentences or a short paragraph. Sometimes I have reversed this sequence, opening with a statement of purpose and following it with an argument articulation; on occasion I have even paraphrased the initially stated purpose after the argument articulation for additional emphasis or clarity.

Of course, you may not work from an outline (many writers do not), so this structure might serve only as a guide when organizing your thoughts in preparation for drafting an article.

Quite honestly, oftentimes I simply sit down at my computer and begin drafting thoughts on a topic I am considering for a practitioner article.

As I begin drafting a paper, I typically get stuck in the introduction, which is the most difficult part of an article for me to write. I will stop and ask myself, "What am I trying to say? What is my purpose for writing this paper?" Then I will employ the "argument articulation/statement of purpose" structure to ferret out my argument. Thus, sooner or later I usually end up challenging myself to make a clear statement about why I am writing an article. When I am able to do this, I generally find that the rest of the drafting stage proceeds fairly smoothly. When I am unable to express a clear argument, I find myself in trouble, and often end up scrapping or modifying the idea. My point is that if you are able to express a clear purpose or thesis for writing a paper—in a sense, convincing yourself that you have something worthwhile to write about—then you will probably be in a better position to convince editors and reviewers that you have something important to say.

Select a Target Journal

Scores of periodicals publish works in literacy education (approximately 150 of them are described in the International Reading Association's *Contributor's Guide to Periodicals in Reading*). Identifying one, or possibly two, target journals for a work you will write is an important prewriting step. Having a specific outlet in mind enables you to tailor your article so that you address the appropriate audience and prepare the manuscript in the prescribed form and style. Doing so enhances the possibility of having your work accepted for publication.

To identify a target journal, peruse various potential targets and determine if they tend to publish pieces that are similar in tone, style, and content to the article you have in mind. For example, if you were planning to prepare an article describing a specific writing activity you have used successfully in your elementary classroom, *Language Arts* would be a logical prospective outlet since this elementary-level journal regularly publishes pieces on composing.

Maribeth and I decided that *The Reading Teacher* would be our first choice for publishing the WWHW article we planned to write. We envisioned a fairly short (10-15 double-spaced manuscript pages), practical piece that addressed elementary reading teachers. The article we planned was very much like many works that were appearing in *The Reading Teacher* at that time, so our choice made sense. In addition, *The Reading Teacher* is the most widely read elementary-level practitioner journal in reading, so we decided we might as well try to get published in the journal with the greatest circulation.

Of course, we knew that our chances of having our work accepted in our target journal were modest at best (the acceptance rate of *The Reading Teacher* was and remains about 10-12 percent), so we discussed other possible outlets in case the article was rejected. In this event, we decided that *Reading Research and Instruction*, *Reading Psychology*, and *Reading Horizons* would be our next choices, in that order.

Once we decided on *The Reading Teacher* as our target journal, we carefully read the most current issues—a crucial step in enhancing the chances for journal article acceptance, as Jensen emphasizes in the preceding chapter. Looking carefully at current issues confirmed for us that a practical article on comprehension instruction was something that might be received favorably by *The Reading Teacher's* reviewers and editors, since the journal was running many articles on similar topics at that time.

Upon further inspection of the journal, it became apparent that the comprehension instruction pieces being published were based either on original research conducted by the authors or on the work of others. Knowing that the WWHW strategy was empirically based, we began to feel good about our chances of having our work accepted. In short, we believed that *The Reading Teacher* was an ideal potential outlet for the paper we planned to write.

Next, we read the section labeled "Contributions" in the front of one of the journal's recent issues. We had already written to the International Reading Association for the *The Reading Teacher*'s "Instructions for Authors" pamphlet, which gave us much detailed information about the preferred substance, form, and style for submission. The brochure and the "Contributions" section also provided us with specific information such as how to prepare references, how to type or print the paper, and how many copies to submit.

This information is fairly mundane, but be assured that preparing a manuscript that conforms precisely to form and style guidelines (and one that is impeccably typed/printed and copied) will enhance its chances for acceptance. Editors and reviewers are most interested in the substance of the papers they handle, but they also are influenced, either positively or negatively, by aesthetic and stylistic qualities. Editors and reviewers become distracted, and perhaps even annoyed, when they recognize that the authors either were unaware of journal form and style requirements or chose to ignore them. In short, you are unnecessarily putting yourself at a disadvantage if your manuscript does not conform exactly to journal guidelines.

Write for Your Target Journal

Composition is a personal, idiosyncratic process; procedures that work well for one author may not be helpful to another. Consequently, there are no prescribed formulas for writing articles for practitioner journals. All I can do is describe a format that has worked well for me. Please note that other ways of organizing and writing articles for practitioner journals can be equally (or more) effective. Your personality, writing experiences, and writing style will dictate the most effective procedures for you.

**Figure 2
One Possible Organization
for Articles in Practitioner Journals**

Introduction
• concise review of relevant literature
• clearly stated purpose/thesis (why your topic is important, interesting, needed)
 – convince editors/reviewers/readers that the topic/information is current, novel, and interesting

Body
• explicit presentation of teaching strategy
• informal, clear, lucid presentation of research methods and results
• examples; rich, illustrative text; visuals or graphics
 – leave reader with a clear sense of what you're describing and how it can be used

Closing
• summary and/or conclusions
• extensions, applications, and limitations

Figure 2 presents an organization I have used successfully when writing articles for practitioner journals. Certainly, the three-part structure of introduction/body/closing is nothing new; much expository writing contains these features in some fashion. This structure is often linked to the old adage that a writer of exposition should "Tell 'em what you're gonna tell 'em; tell 'em; then tell 'em what you just told 'em." This maxim is a bit simplistic, but it does capture the essence of this organization.

Introduction

The introduction presents the argument or rationale for an article. Readers should finish the introduction with a clear sense of why the author wrote the article so they can decide whether to read on for the substance of the strategy, technique, or information presented. I am a firm believer in the value of an explicit purpose statement. Writing "The purpose of this article is..." or "In this article, I will..." or "This article presents..." somewhere in the introduction provides readers with a clear, direct sense of why the article is important and what it is about. When we give authors guidelines for revising works they have submitted to *The Reading Teacher*, we frequently suggest that they reflect on what their thesis or argument is and then include an explicit purpose statement early in the article.

Introductions for practitioner journals should be written concisely. Pare down the review of relevant research and theory on your topic to its most critical, central points. The argument articulation/statement of purpose format described earlier in this chapter has worked well for me when writing introductions; you may also find it or some version of it useful.

You can also be creative when writing introductions. For example, authors sometimes open articles with vignettes: quotations from literature, descriptions of teachers and students, or excerpts from an oral or written protocol. Headings or subheadings are generally not needed in introductions. It is implicit that an article begins with an introduction, so denoting it formally is not required.

Body

The body of an article for practitioners contains the core or essence, the practical information. For example, in the WWHW article, an article that described a strategy for comprehension instruction, we organized the information with the following headings and subheadings:

Four-Step Strategy for Teaching Comprehension Skills
Step 1. WHAT is the reading skill?
Step 2. WHY is the reading skill important?
Step 3. HOW does one use the reading skill?
Step 4. WHEN should the reading skill be used?

An Example
   Step 1. What
   Step 2. Why
   Step 3. How
   Step 4. When

In the first section, we described in general the features of each of the four steps in the strategy. In the second section, we provided an elaborate example of how a teacher might structure a lesson according to this model. The example described a fourth grade teacher who taught a lesson according to the WWHW procedure for identifying and understanding unstated paragraph main ideas.

Of course, many internal organizations are possible. For example, if you were reporting an action research study you conducted in your classroom, you would describe your students and the classroom environment, the type of intervention program you developed, and information documenting the program's effectiveness.

The body of an article for practitioners should be sufficiently detailed and explicit to allow other teachers to try the instructional ideas or adapt them to their own teaching situations. Headings and subheadings may help you organize information and key your organization for readers. Lucid, rich descriptions, examples of students' work, and transcripts or testimonials from students or teachers can help this section come alive.

Figures, drawings, or photos that enhance the narrative are also helpful. For example, in the sample lesson in the WWHW article, we had the teacher use a "Main-Idea-Pede" (a centipede-type bug) to demonstrate the relationship between main ideas and details. The main idea was on the bug's body and details were on its legs, the analogy being that details support main ideas just as legs support a body. We thought the drawing was a little corny at the time, but we knew it worked well with children, and people who liked the article invariably noted how the graphic helped them understand and use the instructional model.

Closing

There are various ways to close an article. In some instances, a simple summary of the major points is appropriate. In other cases, logical conclusions can be drawn. Describing extensions, applications, or limitations of an instructional strategy or applied research study is another option. In the WWHW article, we closed with a section titled "Adapting Commercial Materials," within which we described how our strategy could be used in conjunction with published materials such as basal reading programs or instructional kits and packages. We concluded this section, and the article, with this simple summative statement:

> In conclusion, the What-Why-How-When format gives teachers a simple, yet empirically sound, plan for providing instruction in reading comprehension skills. It accounts for the three basic types of knowledge that are required for successful, independent use of reading skills (Baumann & Schmitt, 1986, p. 646).

As with the introduction to an article, there is no one best way to close an article. However, providing readers a summarization, recapitulation, or extension of what you have said is a reader-friendly means to conclude a piece of writing.

Obtain Presubmission Reviews

Before sending an article off to a journal, it is extremely helpful to get a critical review of the work from a colleague or friend, ideally a person who is an experienced author. Before we sent the WWHW article off to *The Reading Teacher*, Maribeth read my draft with a sharply critical eye. We also asked several colleagues to read the paper. We already had student comments, since we had used an earlier draft as a handout in our reading methods classes. Armed with various constructive criticisms, we made a number of revisions that improved the paper significantly.

The purpose of presubmission reviews is, of course, to enhance the quality of an article so that it is more likely to be received favorably by editors and reviewers and eventually accepted for publication. Although it takes time to obtain this feedback, I have found presubmission comments to be helpful. When obtaining these comments, I ask readers to view my work as if they were rigorous reviewers for my target journal.

Presubmission reviews are helpful only if the reader responds *critically* to the paper. Therefore, friends may not be the best ones to do this. You need someone who is willing to tear a paper to shreds if that represents her or his opinion. You as the author need to be thick skinned as you digest these critical comments. Don't take the criticisms personally. Recognize that if you get candid, astute comments from reviewers who have insight into the process of journal publishing, you ought to be able to revise your work to eliminate problems that might otherwise have resulted in an initial rejection. In short, presubmission reviews can put you one step ahead in the review process.

Revise, Edit, Proofread, and Submit

Many writers state that composition is the most intellectually challenging and exhausting task they undertake. I would certainly agree. There are no short cuts to success, and the most diligent and hard-working writers tend to be the most successful. Some of the hardest work comes at various stages of revision.

Revision is painful, tiring work, but it is essential. I believe that many authors who do not get works published fail because they do not persist with revisions. I have some papers in my files that underwent five or six revisions before they were finally published. Some of those revisions occurred before I submitted the paper, the result of presubmission reviews. Some came after a paper had been rejected outright; the editors did not want to see a revision, but I decided to revise the paper and send it out to another journal. Some came after a paper had been returned by an editor who indicated that a significantly revised paper might be accepted after another round of reviews (but there was no guarantee). Some were the result of a conditional acceptance based on the completion of specific, prescriptive revisions. And some were simply to polish the paper prior to its final acceptance. In all cases, however, each revision improved the clarity of my message. Revision is not enjoyable, but it is productive.

So, synthesize the comments you obtain from your presubmission reviews and rework your paper accordingly. You should not necessarily follow all the suggestions—some advice might be bad—but try to appreciate where you led the readers astray and how they misunderstood your message. Then complete the necessary reorganization, rewording, additions, or deletions to address their concerns.

After you have revised your paper on the basis of the presubmission reviews, it is time to polish your work before submitting it to your target journal. This step involves careful editing of the paper. Use a style manual to guide you in matters of grammar, usage, mechanics, and punctuation. *Elements of Style* by Strunk and White (1979) is my preferred resource, although many other fine handbooks are available.

Many journals prescribe the use of a specific editorial style. The most common style required for reading and language arts journals is that of the American Psychological Association (APA). These style guidelines are published in book form as the *Publication Manual of the American Psychological Association* (1983). If you plan to be a frequent submitter to literacy education journals, purchase your own copy of the APA manual; it is a worthwhile investment. In the case of the WWHW article, we relied on *The Reading Teacher's* "Instructions for Authors" pamphlet for style guidelines, since at that time the journal had its own style (which has since changed to APA style).

Whatever the style is for a journal, follow it *explicitly*. All headings, references, figures and tables, typing and spacing, pagination, abstract preparation, and the like should be exactly as prescribed by the editors or style manual. You want the reviewers of your work to focus on what you have to say, not on stylistic deviations.

Before you send your manuscript off to your target journal, enlist the assistance of a good proofreader. Ask someone strong in English grammar to read the paper for linguistic gaffes such as split infinitives, dangling participles, lack of subject-verb agreement, improper usage, misspellings, and other errors. By the way, the persons who did your presubmission reviews may not be the best choices for this stylistic editing. You want someone who behaves like a picky English teacher and can point out all your form and style errors. Those who read your paper at a more substantive level may not be interested in or particularly skilled at tedious form editing.

When all the editing and proofreading are done, you are ready to type or print your paper. Make certain it is typed or printed as neatly as possible, ideally using a laser printer or a letter quality printer or typewriter. If you have a dot matrix printer, use the near-letter-quality mode. If your typewriter or printer uses a ribbon, insert a new one. Do whatever you can to produce a dark, clear, and easily reproducible manuscript. The aesthetics of a manuscript are very important, as an editor's or reviewer's first opinion of your work is determined not by what your paper says but by how it looks.

Next make the prescribed number of copies (usually three to five) to send to the journal editor. Retain either the original or a clear copy for your records to guard against possible loss of your parcel in the mail. Most journals do not require an original manuscript and will accept instead the appropriate number of photocopies; check the journal style guidelines to be certain.

Assemble the package and prepare a brief cover letter. Most editors do not require an explanatory cover letter (some even discourage them), but a letter may be helpful. In it state briefly what your article is about, why you wrote it, and why you believe that it is especially appropriate for the journal to which you are submitting it. We accept or reject manuscripts for *The Reading Teacher* on the basis of their contents, but we do read cover letters, and sometimes they provide insights or explanations that were not obvious from reading the manuscript itself. In short, a cover letter will do you no harm.

You can mail your manuscript using simple first class mail or its equivalent (registered or certified mail is not necessary). However, international submissions should be posted air mail, as opposed to surface mail, to avoid long delays. *Submit your article to one journal at a time.* This is standard practice, and editors assume that only they are considering your paper. This policy prevents double acceptance of papers, which angers editors and results in wasted editorial and review energy. Most journals acknowledge the receipt of manuscripts (usually within two weeks), so do inquire if you have not received notification of receipt within a reasonable amount of time. Then simply sit back and wait, or begin working on your next writing project.

Celebrate or Revise and Resubmit

When editors receive papers, they screen them to determine whether they are appropriate for the journal. If they are not (i.e., if the content or focus does not match the journal's audience or purpose), or if a manuscript is not in the appropriate style, it will be returned to an author without review. If a paper is appropriate for review, editors generally assign two to four reviewers (three being the usual number) to evaluate it.

Reviewers are selected on the basis of how closely their expertise matches the topic of the paper. They read a paper carefully, express their opinion on a manuscript review form, and return this information to the journal editors. Then the editors read the paper carefully themselves, assemble and synthesize their reviewers' opinions, and adjudicate the paper; that is, they make a decision about whether to publish it. The editors then communicate their response to an author in a letter, enclosing the editorial advisors' reviews. Often, response letters are lengthy and complex, particularly when editors provide an author with detailed suggestions for revising a paper. This entire process takes anywhere from 1 to 4 months, 3 months being the usual standard.

What kind of response might you receive from an editor? The types of editorial decisions editors communicate to authors vary from journal to journal, but frequently the decisions fall into one of four groups. To help you understand what these decisions are and what they might imply for possible revisions, inspect the following manuscript review form (Figure 3), which editorial advisors for *The Reading Teacher* complete for every paper they review.

The review form has three major sections: manuscript rating scale, author comments, and publication recommendation. The rating scale and comments for author sections provide a rationale for the reviewer's publication recommendation. For example, if a reviewer recommends that a paper be rejected, she or he will generally circle low numbers on the rating scale, and her or his comments will explain why the article should not be published (our reviewers often attach one or two additional pages of typed comments for authors). The journal editors then synthesize the information from all the review forms and reach a decision. For *The Reading Teacher*, we give authors a publication decision that corresponds to one of the four choices listed on our review form. Many other journal editors use these same decision categories. For *The Reading Teacher* (and most other journals), these editorial decisions should be interpreted as follows.

Figure 3
Manuscript Review Form for *The Reading Teacher*

The Reading Teacher
Manuscript Review Form

Manuscript No. _____ Reviewer No. _____ Review No. _____

Manuscript Title _____

Date Manuscript Sent for Review _____ Please Return by _____

Manuscript Rating Scale	Poor		Good		Publication Recommendation
Content: important	I	2	3	4	__ Accept for publication
Content: interesting	I	2	3	4	__ Accept conditionally pending the
Content: novel	I	2	3	4	satisfactory completion of
Content: current	I	2	3	4	revisions noted below
Theoretically or empirically based	I	2	3	4	__ Reject in current form, but encourage the author to revise
Appropriate for RT audience	I	2	3	4	and resubmit for another round of reviews
Clear, focused, well written	I	2	3	4	__ Reject for reasons noted below
Other _____	I	2	3	4	

Typed Comments for Author (rationale for recommendation; specify suggestions for revision)

(continue on a separate sheet if necessary)

Reviewer's signature _____ Date _____

(optional)

Return completed review to: *The Reading Teacher*, School of Education, Purdue University, West Lafayette, IN 47907

Accept for Publication

This decision means that a paper is essentially in publishable form and that only minor copyediting is required. If you receive such a response, celebrate, for you are in the distinct minority; it is infrequent that editors recommend outright acceptance of a paper (we accept outright only 1 to 2 percent of all papers submitted to *The Reading Teacher*). We got lucky with the WWHW paper, as we received an acceptance letter without the condition of revision, although we did negotiate changes later when the editor did some substantive copyediting.

Accept Conditionally

This decision means that the editors like a paper and will commit to publishing it if an author is able to make specified revisions. The required revisions may be fairly minor or more substantial—either way, this recommendation is a very positive one. Make the changes the editors suggest and resubmit the revised paper. The editors will review the new version themselves; they may also ask one or two editorial advisors to read and evaluate the revision. If the revised paper is acceptable, the editors will formally accept it for publication. Thus, an accept conditionally decision is a form of contract: If an author can complete some fairly prescriptive revisions, the editors will agree to publish the paper.

What should you do if you find some suggestions for revision illogical or if you disagree with them? I recommend that you revise the paper as *you* see fit. Then write a cover letter explaining why you did or did not make the recommended changes. The editor may still disagree with you and either reject your paper or insist that you make the suggested revisions. Editors are reasonable people, however; in most situations, if your reasoning is sound, they will either concur with your judgment or be willing to negotiate the revisions in question. Remember, the writing is your work, and you must feel comfortable that it expresses what you believe.

Reject in Current Form

The reject in current form (RCF) decision means that the editors see value in your ideas but believe that significant revisions are required. In short, the editors are saying that you have some good ideas in your work, but they need to be extended, modified, or altered substantially for the paper to be acceptable. A revised and resubmitted paper will be reviewed again. Editors typically assign a combination of first-round reviewers and new ones to RCF papers. Second-round reviewers usually receive copies of the first-round reviews, the editors' response letter to you, and your cover letter accompanying the revision, so they have a sense of the history of the paper. (This is our policy at The Reading Teacher for RCF papers.)

The reject in current form decision is a common one (about one-third of first-round submissions to The Reading Teacher receive an RCF). An RCF is not, like the accept conditionally decision, an informal contractual arrangement. However, you should not be discouraged if you receive this verdict. Many papers I have had published were initially rejected by the journal in which they ultimately appeared, and many of the papers we have accepted for publication in The Reading Teacher started out as RCFs.

When you receive an RCF response, you have two choices. One choice obviously is to revise your paper and resubmit it to the same journal. Another is to send your paper to another journal, with or without revising it. Generally, I recommend revising and resubmitting an article to the same journal, as you have a decent chance of having it accepted, either outright or conditionally, if you have done the revisions well. However, if you disagree strongly with the editors' evaluation of your paper, you might consider sending it to another journal. Even in this situation, I suggest that you carefully consider reviewers' and editors' comments and revise your paper; reviewers for a different journal are likely to find the same problems with your paper that the first set of reviewers saw.

Reject

This decision means that the editors have decided they are not interested in publishing your work and they are not inviting you to revise and resubmit your paper to them for further evaluation. This is disappointing news, of course, but all writers—even very successful ones—have had papers rejected.

What should you do when you receive a rejection? Don't give up; instead, go back to the drawing board. Look at the comments of the reviewers and editors. Analyze why they rejected your paper. Was it a conceptual problem? Was your topic not sufficiently important, interesting, or novel? Did you fail to

---

Writing is an art, a craft, not something that can be standardized. ■ ■ ■

---

provide an empirical or theoretical basis? Was the problem with your writing style? After considering these questions, you might decide that your idea is not worthy of publication, or that a major flaw exists in your research or in a line of reasoning. In those cases, it might be best to let a paper die.

In many situations, however, rejected papers can be salvaged through extensive revisions. More than once I have tossed a rejected paper on a table in the corner of my office (or the trash can, although I always fished it out) only to return to it later. Not every rejected paper was a phoenix, but most were ultimately published in some form somewhere (though not necessarily in my first, second, or even third choice of journals). In short, keep the faith. It's normal to be angered or demoralized with a rejection, but it is the resilient, persistent writer who is successful. So, mourn, but only briefly; then return to your work.

Conclusion

In this chapter I have described the process I have used for writing and submitting articles for publication in practitioner journals in reading and language arts, and I hope that aspiring writers find something useful here. Recognize, however, that because this information is personal, it may not be generalizable. The procedures that have worked for me may not be useful to others. Formulas do not exist; these are not seven magic steps.

I should also acknowledge that these thoughts on writing are retrospective; that is, I have reflected on what I have done and then described what I did. I cannot say that I consciously followed this process at the time, nor that I followed it precisely for all writing tasks. Writing is an art, a craft, not something that can be standardized. Painters, sculptors, and musicians express themselves creatively equally well in many divergent ways. So, too, with the process of writing. View my comments as tips, but ultimately I advise you to follow your intuition and to learn from your experiences.

References

Baumann, J.F. (1983). A generic comprehension instructional strategy. *Reading World, 22*, 284-294.

Baumann, J.F. (1984). The effectiveness of a direct instruction paradigm for teaching main idea comprehension. *Reading Research Quarterly, 20*, 95-115.

Baumann, J.F. (1986). Teaching third-grade students to comprehend anaphoric relationships: The application of a direct instruction model. *Reading Research Quarterly, 21*, 70-90.

Baumann, J.F., & Schmitt, M.B. (1986). The what, why, how, and when of comprehension instruction. *The Reading Teacher, 39*, 640-646.

Contributor's guide to periodicals in reading. (updated annually). Newark, DE: International Reading Association.

Publication manual of the American Psychological Association (3rd ed.). (1983). Washington, DC: American Psychological Association.

Schmitt, M.B., & Baumann, J.F. (1986). How to incorporate comprehension monitoring strategies into basal reader instruction. *The Reading Teacher, 40,* 28-31.

Strunk, W., Jr., & White, E.B. (1979). *Elements of style* (3rd ed.). New York: Macmillan.

Weintraub, S. (Ed.). (annually). *Annual Summary of investigations relating to reading.* Newark, DE: International Reading Association.

Publishing in Newsletters and Newspapers

John Micklos, Jr.

Micklos begins this chapter by relating insights he has gained from his experience as a newspaper writer and editor. He then describes outlets for news articles, columns, and features, including the International Reading Association's bimonthly newspaper, Reading Today, *other education newspapers and newsletters, and broad interest newspapers. He includes a description of the unique style required for newspaper and newsletter writing as well as information about how to write articles that will remain coherent even after they have been severely cut by an editor. Tips for overcoming writer's block are also included.*

■ ■ ■ ■

Having looked at newsletters and newspapers from the perspective of both a writer and an editor, I have gained some insight into the specialized needs of these publications. Education newsletters and newspapers often accept articles from people in the field, but their needs and requirements may be quite different from those of the professional journals to which many educators regularly contribute.

Accepting articles from outside writers offers the newsletter editor several advantages:

- A fresh perspective
- Expert knowledge of a specialized field or subject area

- Cutting-edge information
- Ideas that have been tested in a classroom or research setting.

For the prospective writer, newsletters and newspapers offer a chance to write a different type of article in a different style than journals require. Also, the chances of acceptance may be higher among small newsletters than among large journals that receive hundreds or even thousands of submissions annually.

In order to publish in newsletters and newspapers, however, you must keep some general principles in mind, as these publications are quite different from journals in structure and format.

General Principles

Know Your Market

A cardinal rule for writers is that they must familiarize themselves with the publication to which they are submitting material. *Reading Today*, of which I am editor, is the membership newspaper of the International Reading Association; as such, its content focuses on education in general and reading education in particular, with special emphasis on Association activities. Yet you would be amazed by the number of articles I receive that have little or no relationship to reading education.

As noted in Chapter 4, the Association's *Contributor's Guide to Periodicals in Reading* (updated annually) is a good resource for pinpointing possible outlets for your articles. The guide gives an idea of the types of articles published by approximately 150 newsletters and journals. Other resources, such as *Writer's Market* (annually), are available in bookstores and libraries.

When in doubt, write to the editor of the newsletter or newspaper. Some editors have writers' guidelines available, and some will send you a free copy of their publication so you can see the format and style of the articles. *You should never submit an article to a publication you have not read recently.*

Pay Attention to Length Requirements

Length is one of the features that distinguishes newsletter writing from journal writing. While many journals publish articles of 3,000 or more words, the size and format of newsletters/ newspapers dictate that their articles be much shorter. In *Reading Today*, articles may be as short as 200 or 300 words; articles of more than 1,500 words are rarely used. A general rule of thumb for publication in *Reading Today* (and many other newsletters/newspapers) is *the shorter the article, the greater its chances of getting published.*

You should never submit an article to a publication you have not read recently. ■ ■ ■

If your article is lengthy and complex, it is probably better suited for use in a journal. Length requirements vary greatly, however; once again, the best way to ensure that you're on target is to read the newsletter or newspaper or to check the publication's guidelines before submitting an article.

Keep Stylistic Differences in Mind

Some education newspapers and newsletters run articles that are quite similar in style and content to those found in journals. Most, however, focus on stories that are more topical and less research-oriented than those in journals. With this in mind, don't submit to a newspaper or newsletter an article with 30 references.

Most newspapers also use a more conversational style of writing than is found in journals. Newspapers favor active verbs and short sentences and paragraphs. By and large, however, the same rules of grammar and punctuation apply to both types of publications.

Keep Format Differences in Mind

The format of newspaper articles differs considerably from that of journal articles. Newspaper articles generally are written in what is called an inverted pyramid style. This means that the most vital information—the who, what, when, where, why, and how—is included in the first paragraph or two. Subsequent paragraphs focus on progressively less newsworthy background information.

The reason for the prevalence of this format is that newspapers face extremely tight space restrictions, and usually layout is not completed until close to the printing deadline. The inverted pyramid style allows editors to cut off at the bottom enough material to make an article fit its allotted space without altering the most important facts.

On several occasions, articles I've written for newspapers have been published virtually unchanged except that the last few paragraphs have been omitted. This shows the importance of adhering to the inverted pyramid style. Incidentally, I try not to edit that way in *Reading Today*, since I prefer to save space by tightening throughout rather than by cutting out an entire chunk at the end.

Prepare Manuscripts Properly

As with journal submissions, manuscripts for newspapers or newsletters should be neatly typed, doublespaced. You'd be surprised at how many people submit hastily scrawled manuscripts for publication in *Reading Today*, apparently thinking that newspapers and newsletters have lower standards than journals.

Query Letters Can Be Helpful

Most broad-circulation newspapers and magazines prefer query letters to completed manuscripts; sending query letters may also be helpful in dealing with professional newspapers and newsletters. A query letter is a brief summary of the article you are proposing. Reading a query letter gives an editor a chance to see whether a proposed article is appropriate for the publication's audience. Editors also use query letters to help judge whether the author can write effectively. For the author, sending a query letter can prevent investing a lot of time in writing an article that is inappropriate for the targeted publication.

Query letters range in length from one or two paragraphs to a page. An effective query letter describes the idea to be covered, gives a proposed length, states why the author is qualified to write the article, and notes why the article is appropriate for the publication. If the editor agrees that the idea is a good one, he or she will encourage the author to proceed. Often, the editor will have specific suggestions regarding focus, structure, or length. Note that acceptance is almost never guaranteed until the editor sees the finished article.

With especially timely articles, a telephone query may be acceptable. In most cases, however, editors prefer written queries. From personal experience, I know that it is easier to make a carefully considered decision after reading a query letter than after hearing an idea over the telephone.

Dealing with Writer's Block

One of the biggest obstacles in preparing an article is writer's block. Often, the hardest aspect of writing is trying to transfer those wonderful ideas from your head to a blank piece of paper. Writer's block can affect anyone, from first-time writers to bestselling authors. Here are some tips for eliminating the problem.

1. Start with the easiest writing project you have to do. Sometimes that will loosen up your creative juices for the harder projects.

2. If you have a word processor, just start hammering out a draft, no matter how rough or disorganized it may be. Once it's on the machine, editing and reorganizing the material is relatively easy.

3. Try working on the beginning and the ending of the article first. Sometimes the middle will then just fall into place.

4. If you are leaving a project at the end of the day, stop in the middle of a paragraph (or even in the middle of a sentence). When you finish the missing element the next day, you'll have a running start.

5. Take a break. Take a walk. Put the troublesome project aside and leave your desk for a few moments. Sometimes even a brief time away can break the mental logjam.

6. Look at another similar project that you've already completed. Sometimes that will help convince your subconscious that it's really possible to complete the project at hand.

7. Set aside a regular time for writing, and try not to let anything interrupt your writing sessions. If you get accustomed to writing at a regularly scheduled time, you will find that it becomes progressively easier to slip into a productive writing mode during that time.

8. It has been said that writing is 15 percent worrying, 10 percent planning, 25 percent writing, 45 percent revising, and 5 percent proofreading. If we as writers can learn to turn that worrying time into creative time, our potential will be boundless!

Guidelines for Submitting to *Reading Today*

Now let me share some general tips and specific guidelines for submitting articles to *Reading Today*. Keep in mind that although the focus here is on a particular publication, many of these tips can be adapted for submitting material to other reading-related newsletters and newspapers.

General Tips

1. Articles should be of interest to the widest possible segment of the Association's membership.

2. Articles should be written in a straightforward, nonacademic style. We try not to use too many references.

3. We prefer articles that are practical in nature to articles that are research-oriented.

4. The shorter the article, the better chance there is that we can use it. Articles of more than 1,500 words rarely are published. Articles for special sections of the newspaper, such as "News for Parents" and "News for Administrators and Supervisors," are even shorter—about 250-750 words.

Guidelines for Specific Sections

Listed below are the sections of *Reading Today* that most frequently use articles from outside contributors, along with some specific guidelines for each. Unless otherwise noted, articles should be sent to John Micklos, Jr., *Reading Today* Editor, International Reading Association, 800 Barksdale Road, PO Box 8139, Newark, DE 19714-8139, USA.

Letters to the Editor. Did you especially like something you read in *Reading Today*? Did you disagree strongly with something? Let us know. Put it in a concisely stated letter to the editor, and you may find yourself in print. Letters of 400 words or less are the easiest for us to use, and we try to print those letters that we think will be of interest to the widest possible range of Association members. Names are used with all letters.

Commentaries. Commentaries are longer articles (up to 900 words) that allow the author to express a point of view about an issue relating to reading education. We run commentaries on a space-available basis, once again trying to use those that will interest the widest possible audience. Authors receive bylines.

International News. *Reading Today* regularly carries articles relating to important international meetings, activities of Association affiliates, and other topics we think will interest an international audience. Bylines are sometimes given, depending on the length and type of article. As always, the shorter the article, the greater the likelihood that we can use it, but the upper limit is 800 words. Accompanying photos (preferably black and white) are encouraged. We especially welcome information on the activities of Association councils and affiliates throughout the world.

Council News. We sometimes use freelance articles in this section, which is devoted to council events and activities. We are especially interested in brief articles (and photos, if available) relating to innovative council activities. Bylines are sometimes given, depending on the length and type of article (for two- or three-paragraph reports of council activities, bylines usually are not given). Once again, the shorter the better, but 800 words is the limit.

News for Administrators and Supervisors. Articles in this section are brief (250-750 words) and usually focus on specific ways that administrators or supervisors can support a strong school reading program. The key is to focus on a narrow topic that can be covered in the required length. We especially encourage articles in the 250-300 word range. Authors receive bylines.

News for Parents. Articles in this section, also limited to 250-750 words, usually focus on specific ways parents can help their children develop reading abilities and the reading habit.

Once again, the key is to focus on a narrow topic that can be covered in the required space. Specific ideas that parents can easily implement are especially needed. Authors receive bylines.

Reading Today Goes to Class. This section provides practical ideas that teachers at various grade levels can use in the classroom. Columnists are appointed for 1-year terms for each of the six sections: Infant/Preschool, Early Childhood (grades K-2), Intermediate (grades 3-5), Middle School (grades 6-8), Secondary (grades 9-12), and Adult. Three columns appear in each issue, with the Infant/Preschool, Intermediate, and Secondary columns running in one issue and the Early Childhood, Middle School, and Adult columns running in the next.

In 1988, we instituted an annual open call for columnists, soliciting proposals from any Association member interested in being considered. Application details are available from Association Headquarters.

Other News and Feature Articles. Most other news and feature articles are written in-house or solicited from people with expertise in a particular area. For instance, we may ask Newspaper in Education coordinators to write articles describing local Newspaper in Education Week activities. Government or Association officials, council officers, and other prominent figures in reading education also have contributed articles on request.

Although most of our feature articles are solicited, on occasion people send us unsolicited ideas that are right on target. One such article was a feature on William S. Gray in celebration of the hundredth anniversary of his birth. Other writers have covered important international conferences. If you have an idea you think we should consider, please send us a query letter describing it.

In addition, *Reading Today* occasionally issues calls for brief reader submissions on specific topics. For instance, we have run reader responses to Point/Counterpoint articles, classroom anecdotes submitted by readers, and ideas for celebrating the

Year of the Young Reader. Watch the newspaper for details about such opportunities.

If you have questions or need further information, contact *Reading Today* at Association Headquarters. For specific sections of the newspaper, more detailed writers' guidelines are available on request.

Opportunities in Other Newspapers/Newsletters

While most other education-related newspapers are written primarily by staff people, they may occasionally accept articles from outsiders. For example, both *Education Week* and the *Chronicle of Higher Education* use commentaries in which educators express their point of view on a particular subject. Such articles provide a forum for sharing educational philosophies as well as a chance to write in an expressive, persuasive style. The key to success is reading several issues of the publication for which you would like to write. See how these articles are done and try to write yours using the same general format and style.

Local newspapers also may be willing to consider either single articles or regular columns on topics of general interest. For instance, several years ago I had an idea for a monthly column on children's books. The format involved providing brief reviews of several recommended children's books relating to a specific theme, accompanied by a tip for parents on helping youngsters develop a love of reading. I put together a sample column and a list of prospective topics for the first year and scheduled an appointment with the editor of our local weekly paper. I had barely finished describing the idea before he accepted the proposal without even looking at the sample column.

A similar column on children's literature might be a welcome feature at other newspapers. Editors also might be interested in columns on study skills, ways parents can support children in school, or answers to parents' questions. The key in approaching newspapers is to provide a tightly focused idea and evidence of your writing ability. Also remember that newspaper columns are short, generally running 500-1,000 words in length.

If you are successful in placing a column with one local newspaper, you may want to consider sending it to other newspapers as well to increase the audience you will reach. The editors probably will not mind if you do this as long as you do not place the column with a competing newspaper. You should, however, notify the editor of your intentions.

Local newspapers may welcome single articles on special programs or activities within the district's schools. Articles focusing on students or teachers who have won special awards or who have unusual hobbies may be of special interest. Many small newspapers do not have a large enough staff to cover the schools thoroughly and may truly welcome your submissions. Before submitting an article, you should describe your idea to the editor in a letter or over the phone (local newspaper editors are more likely to accept telephone queries than are editors at large newspapers). Be sure to follow any guidelines the editor gives you regarding style or length.

The newsletters of state/provincial reading associations, local councils, and other International Reading Association affiliates offer another outlet for writers. Many of the tips mentioned earlier for *Reading Today* also apply to these publications. These newsletters probably are most interested in articles or columns relating to the geographic area they cover, but they may also be open to articles featuring ideas that worked somewhere else and could be adapted for use in their area.

It is generally considered improper to send the same article to several newsletters at the same time (called simultaneous submission), although newsletters may be less concerned about this than journals. If you do make a simultaneous submission and the article is accepted by one newsletter, you should notify the others that you are removing the article from their consideration. Although many of these newsletters are not copyrighted, it still is not appropriate to have an identical article appear in several places at the same time.

On the other hand, it is perfectly acceptable to adapt the basic ideas from one article and revise them to form new articles for use in different newsletters. You should, however, make enough changes that the article is substantively different from the previously published version.

Keep in mind that what constitutes a substantive change can be open to interpretation, and different editors may view the matter differently. Let's look at an example. Suppose you have written an article about a new strategy for teaching content area reading. If you wanted to submit it to more than one state/ provincial newsletter, at the minimum you would need to change the lead-in and closing to make them applicable to the particular state or province. You should also adapt any examples within the text to make them pertinent to the readers. You might, however, leave the actual information about the strategy the same for each article.

Even with this level of change, you should tell the editor that the article has been adapted from one you have submitted or published elsewhere. You might also let the editor know just what adaptations you have made. This way, the editor can judge whether the article has been changed enough to be appropriate for his or her publication.

Conclusion

Education newspapers and newsletters offer numerous publication opportunities for writers willing to meet their specialized needs. By studying the publications you hope to write for and learning to satisfy their specific requirements, you may be able to rapidly expand your list of credits. And although writing for a newspaper/newsletter may not seem as impressive as writing for a scholarly journal, in many cases you can reach more people through this medium.

References

Contributor's guide to periodicals in reading. (updated annually). Newark, DE: International Reading Association.

Writer's market. (annually). Cincinnati, OH: Writer's Digest Books.

CHAPTER **SIX**

Writing Reviews of Professional and Instructional Materials
Carol J. Hopkins

Hopkins begins her discussion by examining the review of instructional materials as a form of professional writing and identifying some of the ways reading educators use reviews. She then provides guidelines for structuring reviews of professional and instructional materials, using excerpts from published reviews to illustrate her points. Many of the examples come from The Reading Teacher, *of which Hopkins is an associate editor. The chapter ends with suggestions for obtaining opportunities to write reviews for publication.*

■ ■ ■ ■

Writing reviews of professional and instructional materials requires a different perspective from the types of writing described elsewhere in this book. With a review, your purpose is to critique another author's work rather than to write about a topic you've chosen.

The purpose of this chapter is to (1) look at the review as a form of professional writing designed to evaluate the work of one's peers; (2) examine the use of reviews by professionals in the field of literacy education; (3) provide guidelines for writing reviews of professional and instructional materials, along with examples from published reviews; and (4) suggest ways of obtaining opportunities to write reviews for publication.

What Is a Review?

For the purposes of this chapter, a review is a critical discussion of a peer's recently published work. According to Weinrach (1988b), "Reviews are personal, subjective, and critical analyses of an item or an event. They evaluate, inform, and educate, hopefully through lively writing" (p. 175).

This discussion is limited to published reviews of professional and instructional materials of interest to literacy educators. These materials may include professional books, textbooks, research reports, children's books, software packages, and other primary and supplementary materials. Other types of reviews (e.g., reviews of papers for refereed journals, of outlines and sample chapters of unpublished textbooks, or of sample lessons in proposed instructional materials) share common features, but since they are typically used to make publication decisions and not to be published themselves, they are not dealt with here.

What Function Does a Review Serve?

Reviews serve several important functions for both editors and readers of professional journals. From the standpoint of the editor and the professional organization sponsoring a journal, reviews promote the dissemination of new ideas. Reviews also inform the readership of new publications and products without implying endorsement, for it is clearly the opinion of the reviewer, usually a credible professional with expertise on a particular topic, that is being expressed.

For the reader, reviews are one way of keeping abreast of recent publications in the field. Because most reviews contain a summary of the material's content, they often expand the reader's knowledge about the topic. Furthermore, the review may stimulate readers' thinking about a topic and motivate them to explore the subject of the publication more fully (Weinrach, 1988b).

Reviews also allow readers to learn the opinion of a person who is knowledgeable about a given topic. This is useful for both novice and well-informed readers on the subject, for it helps them to better understand or put into perspective the importance of the work being reviewed and its potential contribution to the field. The review permits readers to compare their opinion of the material with those of other professionals.

Finally, reviews are helpful for professionals who need information about a particular topic or advice about specific types of materials. For instance, a student trying to locate resources for a paper he or she is writing, or a media specialist responsible for purchasing media center materials, may turn to reviews for guidance.

Guidelines for Writing Reviews

One need only look at the diversity of reviews in various publications to realize that no formula exists for writing them. However, there are some common features that most readers and editors expect to encounter in a review. With this in mind, the following general guidelines are offered to help structure a review written for publication. Using these guidelines, along with examining recent issues of the publication in which the review will be published, should give you an understanding of the content of this type of review.

Before undertaking the task of writing the review, it is imperative that you become thoroughly acquainted with the materials you will be reviewing. Study the professional book, textbook, or report carefully; read the children's book to kids; try out instructional materials with a group of students of the age and abilities for whom the materials are intended; boot up the computer program and work through it, either by yourself or with students. These activities will prepare you to write your review.

For the most part, these guidelines apply to both professional and instructional materials, although not all suggestions are appropriate for all materials. Excerpts from published reviews are included to provide examples of how the guidelines may be put into practice.

State the Author's Purpose

Readers of a review may be better able to judge the appropriateness of a book for their professional needs if they understand the author's reason for writing it. For example, knowing whether a book is intended as a textbook, a report of research, a description of an instructional program, or a position paper of a professional organization will help readers evaluate the potential usefulness of the material. Otto (1989) accomplishes this task in the review excerpted here:

> Shannon says in his Introduction that his "intention is to show that the reduction of the teacher's role to manager of commercially produced reading materials not only degrades teachers, but also that it reduces school literacy to the completion of materials—in essence, leaving students to develop literacy on their own" (p. xv). And show it he does!
> Without invective and with only the tiniest bit of hyperbole—and that only in places where Mother Theresa herself couldn't have resisted—Shannon presents a reasoned, documented, and superbly presented case to show that basal readers have come to epitomize a scam that's bigger than orthodontics (pp. 128-129).

Any professional group's endorsement or sponsorship of particular material should also be noted in this part of the review. Johnston's (1990) review provides a good example:

> This publication is the final report of an independent review, sponsored by The Southport Institute, of current federal government activities in adult literacy and

what the federal role should, and could, be. The Southport Institute is an independent, nonprofit organization that provides analyses of public policy issues, especially federal social policy. While the need for an outside evaluation of federal adult literacy policy was originally suggested by the Business Council for Effective Literacy, the advisory group working with the Institute to develop this project included business interests and a broad range of literacy experts (p. 320).

Identify the Material's Intended Audience

Tell readers which groups might be attracted to or benefit from the material you're reviewing. Is it targeted toward administrators, classroom teachers, researchers, college students, or primary grade students?

Also address the question of whether the reader needs any prior knowledge or special preparation to comprehend or use the materials. For instance, when children are the intended audience, are they likely to be able to read and understand the work? Can they use the materials independently, or is teacher assistance required? Are the materials inappropriate for any audience? As seen in the following excerpt from Moore and Moore (1990), identifying the intended audience can be accomplished in a simple statement:

> The emergent literacy books by Morrow and Gibson are primarily for an audience of educational practitioners. These two books cover aspects of children's language and thinking in understandable and well illustrated ways (p. 331).

Lyman (1989), on the other hand, not only identifies the intended audience but also discusses the motivation she believes potential readers must possess:

> Classroom teachers, reading specialists, reading tutors, and special education teachers searching for valid ways

of combining instruction and assessment to break low achieving readers out of their cycles of failure will welcome this new text.... The primary audience for this text is the classroom teacher wanting to develop sound instruction and assessment for readers whose below grade level reading is undermining their school achievement. Taylor, Harris, and Pearson present pragmatic ways to implement the instructional strategies and assessment system they describe. Nevertheless, putting their suggestions and recommendations to work will take a definite commitment on the part of the classroom teacher and others interested in changing their teaching and assessment procedures. The approach they present is an integral one. Therefore, it can be implemented on a gradual, but not on a piecemeal, basis. This text is not the proverbial cookbook from which recipes can be selected here and there. Rather, potential users of the authors' advice must be open to thinking through or rethinking what recent research has to say about the reading process; they must also be willing to learn a system for recording, analyzing, and summarizing information from frequent observations of students reading instructional level classroom material and to teach explicitly word recognition, vocabulary, and comprehension strategies (pp. 66-67).

Describe the Content

Most reviews include a summary or description of the material's content. While you should avoid writing a tedious chapter-by-chapter or lesson-by-lesson description, you need to make sure readers know enough about the content to make an informed decision about whether to examine the book or materials, purchase them, or recommend them to a colleague.

Ask yourself, "What should I tell my readers to help them decide whether this publication is something they should pursue further? What do I think people should know about this work?" The following excerpt illustrates a content summary of a professional book:

Whole Language: Inquiring Voices is intended to be a companion to and an extension of Ken Goodman's "Bright Idea" book *What's Whole in Whole Language*. Concerned that whole language is becoming an orthodoxy rather than a vehicle for self-renewal and learning, Watson, Burke, and Harste invite teachers to go beyond current perceptions of whole language by exploring teaching as researching and curriculum as inquiry.

The authors suggest that inquiry differs from simply asking questions. For inquiry to take place in the classroom, five conditions are necessary: vulnerability, community, generation of knowledge, democracy, and reflexivity. These conditions challenge teachers to articulate their implicit theories, take risks, give all student voices a chance to be heard, share ideas, and engage in meaningful reflection.

Nine stories about whole language teachers functioning as researchers in the classroom exemplify inquiring voices at work. Each of these stories demonstrates the potential of curriculum-as-inquiry, and offers teachers a vision of personal and professional empowerment through the process of creating learning agendas with their students. "An Open Letter to Learners" ends the book on a note that summarizes the main points and again invites teachers to become co-researchers with their students in classrooms.

This book reflects the inherent benefits of collaboration as an energizing and generative learning experience. By sharing their agonies over writing, the authors tell how they relearned through each other that reflexivity and humility are vitally important, that continued engagement is empowering, and that writers need a great deal of support and encouragement (Beverstock et al., 1990, p. 595).

Spiegel (1990) summarizes the content of a set of instructional materials this way:

Critical Thinking: Reading, Thinking, and Reasoning Skills, at first glance, appears to be a routine comprehension workbook. It is a six-book program for Grades 1 through 6 that is organized around Bloom's taxonomy of thinking. The first four of Bloom's stages (knowledge, comprehension, application, and analysis) are emphasized in the materials for Grades 1 through 4. The higher level skills of synthesis and evaluation are introduced in Grade 3. For each stage, several different critical thinking skills are taught. For example, analysis includes (among others) the skills of judging completeness, determining relevance, differentiating between abstract and concrete, and identifying the logic of actions.

What makes *Critical Thinking* stand out is the quality of its teachers' editions and the instructional format provided. A complete lesson plan is supplied for each new skill. This five-part plan includes defining the skill, identifying the steps of the thinking process to be taught, demonstrating the skill through teacher modeling, practicing the skill using the workbook pages, and providing feedback, a step that includes a metacognitive component asking the children to describe what they did to arrive at their answers. Last of all, a section called "Transfer the skill" suggests enrichment activities. In addition, complete annotations appear in the margins of the workbook itself, reminding the teacher to explore the children's thinking and discuss their reasons for rejecting the wrong solutions (pp. 410-411).

One way of determining how much of a summary to include is to think about your audience's prior knowledge of and experience with the material's subject matter. For instance, if you were reviewing a book about a model reading program (e.g., Reading Recovery), you'd need to provide a description of the program because many readers might be unfamiliar with it.

On the other hand, if you were reviewing a book written to help parents become more involved in the school reading program, you might assume that your readers have more experience with the topic and thus go into less detail in explaining the book's content.

It may be helpful to heed VanTil's (1986) advice when writing the summary portion of your review:

> Most readers of the review will never get around to reading the book itself. Sometimes the review is the only estimate of that particular book—and of the author—that a reader will ever encounter. Some readers may intend to read the book; the review may determine whether they do. The reviewer has an obligation to call to their attention books that are worth their while and worth their time investment. Sometimes the book reviewer can happily introduce them to an author who deserves recognition, or to ideas whose time has come (pp. 94-95).

Compare the Material with Similar Works

Readers will want to know what's new or novel about the work under review. When appropriate, compare the book or materials with similar works. Does the material provide any new insights? Is it an extension of or a departure from this author's past work? The authors of the following three excerpts answer these questions:

> Each individual essay, as with all Smith's work since *Understanding Reading* (1971), is wonderfully readable and filled with exquisitely fashioned insights. Like the poet (or the computer) Smith tilts concepts, revealing to the reader fresh perspectives, even when the topic is familiar. However, the veteran reader of Smith's work may find it difficult to glean new insights from information that has already appeared in more depth and brilliance in *Insult to Intelligence* (1986) or elsewhere in Smith's writings (Ewoldt, 1989, pp. 70-71).

A final comment about *Beginning to Read* relates to a summary of it prepared at the Center for the Study of Reading. The summary contains the main points of the original, but, due to space limitations, leaves out most of the examples, analogies, and personal insights that make the unabridged report informative and engaging. Busy educators will appreciate the succinctness of the summary, but the full report gives a much better understanding of and appreciation for the complexity of the topic (Cunningham, 1990, p. 679).

Readers unfamiliar with Shannon's earlier work might find *Broken Promises* difficult. Shannon examines reading instruction from a perspective rarely seen in the reading education literature. Furthermore, he covers much ground quickly. Many assertions require additional support and clarification to be fully grasped—much less accepted. Indeed, readers who want profound criticisms of basal readers probably should begin with *Report Card on Basal Readers*...before delving into *Broken Promises* (Moore & Moore, 1989, p. 253).

State Your Opinion

Most people are asked to write reviews because of their knowledge of, experience with, or expertise in the work's topic, so it is essential that you evaluate the materials and state your professional opinion of them. In order to evaluate material effectively, it's useful to accompany your opinion with the following information.

Identify the evaluation criteria. Because no standardized criteria exist for evaluating professional books and materials, as a reviewer you must determine your own criteria and then inform your readers of them. Let readers know whether you are evaluating the book or materials on the basis of their importance, the timeliness of the ideas, their appropriateness for a particular audience, their potential interest to readers, or their use in a classroom.

Examples of reviews that explicitly state and define the evaluation criteria used may be found in the "Instructional Resources" departments edited by Spiegel in Volumes 43 and 44 of *The Reading Teacher*. The following excerpt, from Spiegel's (1989) column titled "Content Validity of Whole Language Materials," is included to illustrate how evaluation criteria may be included in a review:

> Based on our criteria, *The Whole Language Sourcebook* has high content validity. The focus is on enjoying meaningful pieces of literature and poetry rather than on learning to identify words. "Old Favorites"—familiar pieces of literature—and "New Stories" are used to explore literature in a variety of ways. An extensive bibliography of suitable books or stories is given. Nearly all of the routines include reading, writing, listening, and speaking; they also provide many opportunities for children to work cooperatively in shared learning experiences. Word recognition is fostered through word play, predictable books, and the children's own writing. Reading and writing are used for the authentic purposes of enjoyment, sharing, and learning about the world. Ideas for categorizing, brainstorming, theme notebooks, using calendars and diaries, and incorporating graphs and charts are given both in the Routines and in the Themes sections. The authors are explicit that the themes not be viewed as prescriptions but as models for teachers to use in developing their own units. Within the themes described, activities are not sequenced other than through convenience. Each subsection of Routines describes how to modify that routine (pp. 168-169).

Judge the author's ability to fulfill stated objectives or reader expectations. In your opinion, does the book or material successfully accomplish the author's purpose for writing it? From a reader's standpoint, did it meet your expectations or satisfy your purpose for reading it? Hoffman (1988) addresses these questions in the following excerpt from his review:

> In any review of a research monograph or a research report, standards are applied and judgments are made. On the one hand, it may seem unfair to bring these kinds of lofty standards for research to bear in a review of a study like the ETS Collaborative Research Project on Reading. I certainly do not read the typical journal article or technical report with the expectation of finding a classic work every time. On the other hand, this study, reported in a book format, represents the kind of monumental effort and focusing of resources that one associates with ground-breaking research. Indeed, the authors' stated goals of developing a theoretical proposition about learning to read by drawing on qualitative and quantitative research traditions raise the reader's expectations dramatically. My disappointment with the report stems from my high expectations, not from any inherent flaws in the research itself (p. 387).

Evaluate the material's contribution to the professional literature. In your opinion, how does the book contribute to the professional literature related to its topic? The following excerpt (Tierney, 1989) answers this question explicitly:

> Taken together, the contributions to this volume bring to the surface some of the most pressing concerns as well as key unanswered questions on the teaching of writing. I applaud the editors and authors for the vitality of their contributions. I encourage those of us interested in literacy education to read the volume and consider the challenges presented. I commend the National Society for the Study of Education for sponsoring the volume and entreat them to entertain more frequent forays into written literacy issues. Over 50 years have passed between the present release and the previous yearbook on the teaching of writing. Perhaps other volumes could address not only the changing status of writing but also the movement away from viewing writing as separate from reading, and both as separate from learning (p. 95).

Putting the Pieces Together

The excerpts provided thus far illustrate individual components of a review, but since they cover different types of professional books and materials, it's hard to envision what a single review incorporating these components might look like. The following review of a series of videotapes titled *Showing Teachers How* is provided in full as an example of how these components fit together.

> In 1986, Jeannette Veatch, an internationally known reading educator and longtime advocate of non-commercial instruction, released a series of videotapes that has provided educators with alternative classroom strategies. A second series, comprised of six tapes to date, is now available. These tapes cover a wide range of interesting topics that includes whole language, key vocabulary instruction using an adaptation of Sylvia Ashton-Warner's approach, individualized reading, communication skills in kindergarten children, approaches for using newspapers in the classroom, and inventive strategies for personalizing mathematics instruction.
>
> The tapes are a must for teachers desiring to improve their classroom teaching strategies and for educators involved in teacher preparation programs. Because the topics covered are diversified, they can be easily integrated into undergraduate and graduate coursework. For example, the section on Content Area Reading can be supplemented with *Original Story Problems in Math* and *Newspapers in the 7th Grade*; also, *Communication in the Kindergarten* and *Beginning Reading According to Kierstead* are possible selections for the section on beginning reading. Although each tape focuses on one grade level, the suggestions and ideas can be applied to all grade levels.
>
> Both experienced teachers taking graduate coursework and undergraduate students starting their teacher training program react enthusiastically to the tapes and consider them an accurate depiction of class-

room situations. These inservice and preservice teachers feel the tapes are highly credible because they are well planned, but not rehearsed. Seasoned teachers are more likely to incorporate alternative techniques presented in the tapes into their teaching because they witness the successful implementation of such techniques in a real-life classroom. Moreover, since the tapes illustrate a slice of classroom life, follow-up discussions have evolved around such topics as classroom management, grouping patterns, questioning techniques, discipline, and the pupil-teacher conference. The tapes help bridge the gap between theory and the reality of the classroom. Viewing the tapes enables the undergraduate student to anticipate the reality of classroom life before their upcoming field-based placements and gives them more confidence. When shown during the practicum experience, the tapes allow the student to compare and contrast two different classroom situations.

A unique feature of the tapes is the introduction and summary statements. At the beginning of each tape Veatch offers background and rationale highlighting the important aspects of the upcoming techniques and approaches. Throughout the tape, Veatch interjects insightful comments and presents written subtitles that allow the viewer to coordinate the instructional session with the information presented previously. Her summary statements enable teachers to integrate and review the information.

In summary, Veatch has composed a series of videotapes that can significantly improve reading instruction. Covering a timely range of topics, each lesson is presented by a topnotch teacher who demonstrates clearly how to implement the unique aspects of each teaching strategy. The organization of each lesson is excellent and enables the viewer to follow easily how the major components correlate with its theoretical basis. Veatch has realized her goal of presenting classroom teachers with alternatives to the pervasive and stultifying commercialization current in American schools. By offering these series of videotapes, Veatch has made a significant and lasting contribution to the improvement of reading instruction. The series of 16 programs (US $49.95 apiece) are available in VHS format (Wiesendanger, 1989, pp. 65-66).

Opportunities for Writing Reviews

Editors of journals that publish reviews of professional and instructional materials receive numerous review copies from publishers who hope to give their materials broad exposure. Even though the amount of journal space devoted to reviews is minimal, editors are usually on the lookout for potential reviewers. Sometimes an editor will solicit reviews from educators with relevant areas of expertise. More often than not, however, it's up to you to let editors know of your interest in writing reviews for their journals. The following suggestions will help improve your chances of having reviews accepted for publication.

Authors, editors, and readers alike expect reviewers to be fair and well informed. ■ ■ ■

First, determine which journals publish reviews of professional or instructional materials. The International Reading Association's *Contributor's Guide to Periodicals in Reading,* which provides a listing of periodicals that consistently carry materials about reading, includes a special category to indicate those that publish reviews.

Next, determine the journals you're interested in and write a letter to the editor offering to review particular kinds of materials. In your letter, call attention to any special qualifications you have that might help the editor determine whether to invite your help. Be sure to include a résumé or curriculum vita that details your experience and highlights any professional writing you've done. This way, if the editor decides to accept your offer, he or she will be able to assign the materials you'll review on the basis of your areas of expertise.

Summary

Reviews serve a variety of functions. They may inform, educate, advise, stimulate, or motivate those who read them. They allow writers to discuss, analyze, and evaluate the work of their peers.

Most reviews contain a statement of the author's purpose for writing the material, a summary or description of the contents, the reviewer's opinion, and a statement of how well the book or materials fulfill the author's objectives for writing them. Authors, editors, and readers alike expect reviewers to be fair and well informed in their evaluations and to present their descriptions and impressions with a balance of objectivity and subjectivity (VanTil, 1986).

Perhaps the task of writing reviews is best summed up by Weinrach (1988a): "For obvious reasons, reviewing is no easy task. It requires careful attention to detail, sensitivity to language and meaning, good analytical skills, writing ability, and a modicum of chutzpah" (p. 187).

References

Beverstock, C., Bintz, W., Farley, T., Copenhaver, T., & Hughes, T. (1990). Review of "Whole language: Inquiring voices." The Reading Teacher, 43, 595.

Contributor's guide to periodicals in reading. (updated annually). Newark, DE: International Reading Association.

Cunningham, P. (1990). Review of "Beginning to read." The Reading Teacher, 43, 679.

Ewoldt, C. (1989). Review of "Joining the literacy club." Reading Research and Instruction, 28, 69-71.

Hoffman, J.V. (1988). Review of "Inquiring into meaning: An investigation of learning to read." *Journal of Reading Behavior, 20,* 384-389.

Johnston, J.D. (1990). Review of "Jump start: The federal role in adult literacy." *Journal of Reading, 33,* 320.

Lyman, B.G. (1989). Review of "Reading difficulties: Instruction and assessment." *Reading Research and Instruction, 28,* 66-69.

Moore, S.A., & Moore, D.W. (1989). How to choose and use basal readers—if you really want them. *The Reading Teacher, 43,* 252-253.

Moore, S.A., & Moore, D.W. (1990). Emergent literacy: Children, parents, and teachers together. *The Reading Teacher, 43,* 330-331.

Otto, W. (1989). Wasted days and wasted nights. *Journal of Reading, 33,* 128-130.

Spiegel, D.L. (1989). Content validity of whole language materials. *The Reading Teacher, 43,* 168-169.

Spiegel, D.L. (1990). Critical reading materials: A review of three criteria. *The Reading Teacher, 43,* 410-412.

Tierney, R.J. (1989). Review of "The teaching of writing." *Journal of Reading Behavior, 21,* 91-95.

VanTil, W. (1986). *Writing for professional publication.* Needham Heights, MA: Allyn & Bacon.

Weinrach, S.G. (1988a). If it walks like a review and talks like a review, it must be a review. *Journal of College Student Development, 29,* 187-188.

Weinrach, S.G. (1988b). Reviewing the review process: A critical reassessment. *Journal of College Student Development, 29,* 175-180.

Wiesendanger, K.D. (1989). Review of "Showing teachers how." *Reading Research and Instruction, 29,* 65-66.

PART **TWO**

Publishing
Materials
for Children
and
Adolescents

■ ■ ■ ■

Where Bushes Are Bears: Writing for Children

Myra Cohn Livingston

In this chapter, Livingston provides a personal, emotional view of what it means to write for children. She offers no formula for writing other than devoting oneself to hard, lonely, and oftentimes frustrating work. She argues that writing must be a passion, something one loves to do and cannot live without. In addition, she says, writers need patience, persistence, devotion, and a burning interest in the subject of composition. Livingston speaks from personal experience: a nationally known poet, author, anthologist, and educator, she has written or edited more than 60 books.

■ ■ ■ ■

When Jim and Dale invited me to write this chapter, they asked me to provide practical information, from an author and poet's point of view, about how to write books for children. It probably goes without saying that practicality is not necessarily the hallmark of a poet; in fact, I would suggest that practicality and the writing of poetry are antipodal.

Fortunately, I consider myself to have something of a split personality: one part of me living in the world of imagination where bushes are bears and power lines a great gathering of giant robots; the other, because of experience and fortuitous circumstances, able to turn that world of imagination into poems, anthologies, book reviews, filmstrips, articles, and books. It occurs to me, looking over the table of contents of this book, that the only aspect of publishing into which I have never ventured is that of computer software, explained by the fact that I still write either with a pen or on an ancient Olympia typewriter and understand little about computers.

There are some wonderful perks, however, for those of us who have crossed over the mark of middle age and were not born into a computerized world. I recall watching a program honoring Queen Elizabeth on the occasion of her 60th birthday, during which she spoke of the ideals of her salad days and how she has held to them. Since Elizabeth is only 3 months older than I, I cannot help but feel a distinct bond with her. It is comforting to have a world figure against whom one can measure one's age and life. I, too, have not knowingly compromised the ideals of my salad days. This is not to say that all I have done is sterling, but rather that it was, at its time, the best I could do.

I have a friend who, many years ago, had a contract with a major publisher for a book of essays. Because she envisioned herself writing the finest book of its kind, a book no other author might aspire to produce, she never wrote it. That is excellence carried to a ridiculous extreme. Nevertheless, we must be guided by some standards by which we measure ourselves, first as beginning writers and later as established authors striving to grow and avoid the trap of repeating ourselves over and over again.

The Publication Dream

I suspect that many of you are still in your salad days— either in age or in outlook—with a glimmering, a splendid idea, or a manuscript you wish to give to children as your story, your vision of the world, your contribution to the growth or amusement or education of the young. I think I know how you feel. I was once in that position, and in my writer's program classes at UCLA I am in touch with aspiring authors who work and dream, who write and rewrite and submit pieces, sometimes successfully, sometimes not. I receive letters and manuscripts weekly from fledgling poets asking for a critique; I can envision them putting their work into the mailbox and going through the wretched agony of waiting for some positive response. Actually, even now, with many books published, I still go through this agony. It never ends.

If you don't LOVE to write,
if you can live and breathe
happily WITHOUT
writing, leave it now! ■ ■ ■

It is the poet side of you that dreams of being published, that sees a book with your title, your name on the jacket; perhaps you go so far as to imagine ecstatic reviews, a publication party, being asked for autographs. Today many aspiring authors want even more—an advertising campaign, TV appearances, trips to distant cities, accolades, and even idolization. I do not understand the desire to be a media figure, because if one is busy being such a personality, there can scarcely be the needed time for writing. But I do understand the publication dream.

How to make those dreams reality? Dreams don't come true overnight, and, to be practical, they don't happen without a lot of work. I have spent enough years at my profession to know that writing takes a great deal of work, painful work that can be all-consuming and that leaves little time for frivolities. Writing is a taskmaster. I might go so far as to offer the advice that if you don't *love* to write, if you can live and breathe happily *without* writing, leave it now! For a writer is haunted 24 hours a day by words and ideas and the problems of putting them all together.

But if you are willing to work hard, and if you *must* write—if it makes you a better, more fulfilled person—go to it! Most people, however (unlike Emily Dickinson), want some affirmation that what they write is worthwhile. It's a sort of necessary ego builder. So they decide to try for publication. But what do they do first to confirm that they have something unusual, fresh, vital to offer?

An Individual Voice

Many of my students belong to writers' groups, such as the Society of Children's Book Authors or its spinoffs. They attend conferences and meetings; they find a small number of like-minded individuals who get together for a few hours and read their work to one another. They ask for feedback and critique each other's work. I am of two minds about this type of interchange, for although I suppose it is pleasant to receive compliments or take constructive criticism on the chin, I believe this sort of effort may boomerang. I honestly doubt, for example, whether among such a group anyone is going to castigate the work of a friend, or even an acquaintance. Beginning writers are neither editors nor critics.

More urgently, I feel that writing is the expression of an individual voice, a way of looking and reacting that is unique to one person. If many people express their opinions, urging the writer to add here or delete there, the work is no longer that of an individual but of many people. The writer's vision, style, and purpose is often lost. Collaboration may work well in some situations, but only within certain limits. For example, when I work as a poetry consultant for textbooks, I select the poetry and pass it on to others to decide how best to present it. The taste in selection is mine; I am responsible for it; but it does not purport to be my vision. When we speak of a fine story or an excellent poem, we are looking for a specific viewpoint, a style, a fresh voice.

I would therefore caution aspiring writers to work alone, to make their story or novel or essay or biography the best, as an individual statement, that can be done. My own way of working is to finish a piece and sometimes share it at home, but even that can be of moot value. I remember the day I wrote the poem "The Sun is Stuck" for A *Crazy Flight and Other Poems* (Livingston, 1969), and read it to my family:

> The sun is stuck.
> I mean, it won't move.
> I mean, it's hot, man, and we need a red-hot
>   poker to pry it loose,
> Give it a good shove and roll it across
>   the sky
> And make it go down
> So we can be cool,
> Man.

My husband, my two sons, and my daughter all looked at me as though I had lost my mind. "That's awful," said one. Another explained, "It's not you. You don't talk like that. Leave it out."

I'm glad I didn't take their advice, because the poem has been reprinted four dozen times since, and practically speaking, it has provided us with any number of little luxuries. So much for the opinions of friends and family.

Patience and Perseverance

Teachers and editors, on the other hand, can be of help. As a freshman at Sarah Lawrence College, I found myself in Katherine Liddell's introductory writing class. Her first assignment—no doubt to find out what we knew—was to use onomatopoeia, alliteration, and repetition in some form. What came out of me was a group of about 15 verses. When I went for my weekly conference in Miss Liddell's office, a small converted closet reeking of Sano cigarettes, Miss Liddell informed me that I had written poems for children and should send them to the magazine *Story Parade*.

Of course, I was insulted. I didn't want to write verse for children; I wanted to write great love poetry. I told her I wasn't interested. She said I had better be interested if I intended to stay in her class. I informed her I hadn't the foggiest notion of how to send things to be published. She provided me with all the information. So I sent off the poems with a stamped, self-addressed envelope, and a week later found the fat envelope back in my mailbox. It was as full as before and I threw it, unopened, into a desk drawer. At our next conference, I informed Miss Liddell, with glowing satisfaction, that she had been wrong. The poems had been returned. What did the letter say, she asked. I didn't know, I told her. I hadn't opened the envelope.

About three weeks later, still angry with Miss Liddell, I ripped open the envelope to show her the letter, and caught my breath. The editor had clipped and bought three of the poems. The first, "Whispers," became the title poem of my first book, which was published 11 years later by Margaret McElderry, an editor who had seen the collection that I wrote as a freshman and encouraged me to continued writing.

I tell you this story to illustrate that some people can help once your ideas have left your head and appeared on paper, as well as to highlight the necessity for patience. One often has a manuscript whose time has not come. I tell it also to prove that perseverance is important. During the 11 years between the writing of *Whispers and Other Poems* (Livingston, 1958) and its publication, I sent numerous poems to magazines and was constantly rejected.

I believe that a huge percentage of people have creative potential that is never realized, often because they lack the energy to do the work, but just as often because they give up at the first or the tenth rejection. No doubt there are those who achieve instant success; one thinks of rock stars or movie idols or sports figures. But writing trade books is another matter. The work is hard and lonely. But it is also the headiest, most exciting, and most rewarding work there can be, and I would not trade with anyone in the world. I could not do anything else.

Although I stumbled into writing for children, the publication of Whispers felt very good. In my circle of Dallas friends (who knew me only as a bridge and canasta player) I was somewhat of an oddball, but they tolerated me. Fortuitously, Whispers copped an honor award in the New York Herald Tribune Spring Book Festival, and a number of the poems were reprinted quickly. Now I had not only a wonderful family, but also a book; what more could one ask?

Joy and Protest: Conceiving of Ideas

Jim and Dale asked me to be not only practical (and I've wandered off of that for a moment) but also helpful in addressing the subject of how to conceive of, propose, and implement projects. The fact is that the projects—in this case, the books— seemed somehow to conceive of *me*.

Whispers was written about my own childhood in Omaha, Nebraska, a seemingly happy time albeit in the midst of the Depression. The poems spoke of swings, sliding, sand piles, nature, and the joy of play. At 18 I was quite close to that childhood. By the time Whispers came out I was in my late 20s, but I now had my own children, and watching them prodded my memory of childhood.

My second book, Wide Awake (Livingston, 1959), was dedicated to my son Josh and addressed his world of trucks, bugs, and preschool activities. My early rhythmic prose books all found their beginnings in watching my children and noting how their activities mirrored my own early days. One book, *See What I Found* (Livingston, 1962), was the direct result of my anger over battery-operated toys the boys wanted that fell to pieces after a few days.

Protest against that which annoys or bothers us may be a larger part of writing than one initially suspects. Looking back now I recognize that a number of the books I've written have stemmed from a sizzling and constant anger. Some of this anger came out innocently enough as a book title; *4-Way Stop and Other Poems* (Livingston, 1976) took its title from my annoyance with the traffic department of the community where I live. The reasons behind "Only a Little Litter" are self-evident when one remembers the moon landing that occurred at the time we were trying to clean up America's highways:

> Hey moonface,
> man-in-the-moonface,
> do you like the way
> we left your place?
> can you stand the view
> of footprints on you?
> is it fun to stare
> at the flags up there?
> did you notice ours
> with the stripes and stars?
> does it warm you to know
> we love you so?
> moonface,
> man-in-the-moonface,
> thanks a heap for the rocks.

Equally clear is the motivation behind the words of Arthur, one of a group of black friends, who says in *No Way of Knowing: Dallas Poems* (Livingston, 1980):

When Kennedy
Come to our town
He come with dreams
Got shot right down.

It rained all morning.
You can bet
They didn't want him
Getting wet.

They put a bubble
On his car
So we could see him
From afar.

But then the sun
come out, so they
Just took that bubble
Clean away.

When Kennedy
Come to our town
Some low-down white folks
Shot him down,

And I got bubbles,
I got dreams,
So I know what
That killing means.

I was obviously not invited to write this chapter to share poetry, yet these two examples, I hope, will provide some clues as to how I (and you) conceive of ideas. Attempting to mirror the joy of young children, I wrote my first books; later, protest against many facets of the world—pollution, bigotry, unnecessary mechanization, poverty, autonomous imagery without communication—led me to new ways of seeing and writing. Indeed, I rewrote *Whispers* about 5 years ago as *Worlds I Know* (Livingston, 1985), coming back to that same childhood with a mature understanding of its reality, its devils. Our daughter's childhood led me to see the world from the viewpoint of a girl growing up to a wider choice of options than I had known.

Contact with colleagues can also generate ideas. For example, a few of my books have been conceived at conferences. And it was at a symposium in Berkeley that a colleague asked me why I didn't collect the poetry I loved into an anthology. The idea had never occurred to me, but this chance question resulted in my first anthology, *A Tune Beyond Us* (Livingston, 1968). The collection mirrored my own belief that while we like to call ourselves a melting pot in this country, too often we ignore the work of poets in other countries and of our own black and other minority writers. I wanted to show children that Li Po in eighth-century China abhorred war as deeply as Frank Horne in twentieth-century America; to stress poets' similarities rather than their differences. I wanted to show young people what poems look like in their original languages as well as in translation. Some 26 anthologies later, I still insist that all peoples be reflected in the poetry used.

Today, I look backward and realize that the ensuing anthologies were the result of my work sharing poetry in schools with children, perhaps even a way of allowing myself to stop carrying bagfuls of books or sheets of paper. I've edited anthologies of parody, of humor, of love, of mystery, and of friendship. Most recently I've begun commissioning work for a series of anthologies with holiday themes. I enjoy my role as editor, working with new poets and giving them an opportunity to publish along with more established writers. Perhaps this is the result of my years of teaching, both as poet-in-residence in various schools and at UCLA.

There is no question that teaching has affected my life deeply. It enabled me, once my children were in school during the day, to share with other children my joy in poetry. It also led me to write my first book for adults on the subject of creative writing, *When You are Alone/It Keeps You Capone* (Livingston, 1973), as well as *The Child as Poet: Myth or Reality?* (Livingston, 1984)— which took 25 years to research and 3 years to write—and *Climb Into the Bell Tower: Essays on Poetry* (Livingston, 1990). Teaching also led to the conception of a filmstrip series, *The Writing of Poetry* (Livingston, 1981), which spreads my ideas farther than I can spread myself.

In his poem "The Waking," Theodore Roethke (1966) has a line I have carried with me for years: "I learn by going where I have to go." It is certainly true for me, and I suspect it is true for all of us. A class assignment leads to verses; verses spur one to write a book; publication develops confidence that one's ideas can be shared with others; self-confidence leads to acceptance when one is asked to speak and to teach; teaching results in other books; and eventually, through writing articles and speaking, one is establishing standards for poetry and education that are recognized, by some, as a way of helping young people grow. There are perks, as I mentioned before, for surviving and for cheerfully bearing one's wrinkles.

Working with Publishers

The first publisher contact is, of course, important. Assuming that you have an idea, have worked to give it birth, and are ready to present it, make sure the publisher you choose is one who will be receptive to the type of book you have written. Many people spin their wheels, unsure of where to send a manuscript. While writers' magazines may help, it is always best to spend time in a library or a bookstore noting the sorts of books a publisher favors. Some companies for example, do not publish poetry; others lean toward picture books or teenage novels. My first contact with Harcourt occurred when Mr. Harcourt, on a visit to Sarah Lawrence, suggested that I write to Margaret

McElderry about *Whispers*. Years later, the head of the Children's Room at the Dallas Public Library advised me to try again with the book and gave me the same editor's name. "But I can't send it to her," I protested. "She saw the manuscript years ago." "Do it anyway," she insisted. And I did.

Establishing a relationship with one editor can benefit both sides. Margaret McElderry and I have always had a wonderful relationship. In about 1970 Thomas Y. Crowell published a poets' series and one day, disturbed that Lewis Carroll was not among the poets chosen, I wrote to the editor suggesting that he be included. A letter came back asking me if I would do the book. I was flattered beyond belief, but I got Margaret's blessing before accepting, for those were the days of allegiance to one's editor and publisher. When Margaret moved to Atheneum I followed her; the books I wrote seemed always to be for her list. In 1980, I forged a separate relationship with Margery Cuyler of Holiday House. Since that time Margery and I have worked on 20 books together, with more to come.

I have been approached by other publishers. In some cases, I have said yes because the type of book proposed was not the sort either Margaret or Margery publish. For the most part, however, I work with one of those two editors.

I usually finish a book before sending it off to a publisher, although on occasion I write a proposal first. The filmstrip series came out of a proposal; this series stemmed from my horror at seeing earlier filmstrips that were, to my mind, poorly conceived and just as poorly executed.

The work I have done as a poetry consultant for textbook publishers did not come from any impulse of my own. I remind you again that anyone crazy enough to devote a lifetime to poetry and children and persistent enough to remain a survivor is entitled at a certain point to be asked rather than do the asking. The consulting work is an extension of my own poetry and teaching, but most of all it is rooted in my passion to give children good poetry, good literature.

The Possibility of What Can Be

All this is, of course, not so much to tell you about myself, but to give you an idea of the variety of streets and byways traveled by those who write trade books. I am never certain I should have so many projects. I keep promising myself a month off. And yet in truth, I doubt if I'd like it. There is never enough time to do all we wish, and I expect to die with at least 25 things undone.

I am never certain how much the done things matter; what feeds a writer, I believe, is imagination—the possibility of what can be, what could be. These possibilities are yours to seize. I doubt whether many people claim poetry for their passion, but certainly each of you has some burning interest, some belief about living, some joy or anger that can be translated into your own voice for the young.

In her 1968 Hans Christian Andersen Medal acceptance speech (excerpted here by permission), the Australian writer Patricia Wrightson expresses beautifully some of the ways I feel about my own career and those of friends:

> I feel so very special, so extremely lucky. I must, I think, be one of the luckiest writers who ever lived.... I was lucky as a nervous, fumbling beginner, in daring only to write for [my] children; it took me by accident into the field where the qualities I value count most. I was lucky in stumbling into this field at the moment when it was bursting with life: when the whole small community connected with children's books was concerned and hopeful and purposeful.... That was a wonderful time to begin, when children's books were a sort of mission and every new writer a fresh hope....
>
> I have been lucky and we have all been lucky. We have been wanted and encouraged, given freedom to develop, in a field that is itself a challenge. For this is the field in which to struggle for directness, sharpness, and clarity...it is the field of integrity, where a writer's self-indulgence is least likely to be tolerated; where a

mere sense of responsibility forces one to look again at all one's preconceptions and struggle toward balance and truth. All of these disciplines should surely apply to any field of writing. I have not always felt that they did.

Perhaps other writers have felt the same way. Perhaps they chose for themselves the field into which I stumbled, and began the rich development we've seen for 30 or 40 years. I've often wondered about this: Which came first, the hen or the egg? Did the field, by its potential strength, attract those writers of quality? Or did their quality supply the strength?

Not alone, at any rate. There were all those people who established the climate in which we lucky writers have worked: editors, teachers, librarians, lovers of children, lovers of reading; the small, caring community that stretched around the world...and I want to thank that community, for all of us.

I feel sad that the wonderful time may be coming to an end. Perhaps it is natural to feel like that while the publishing world is in such a state of flux: one never knows, as the takeovers go on, who will be one's publisher next week or which total stranger will be in the editor's chair. One does know that the policy will be to generate the largest possible cash flow, relying on the chosen formula.

There is nothing new in a publisher's need for a cash flow or formula. It is new only when the need for cash is mechanized, automated, and made total, leaving no room for anything except the formula. When that happens, it is no wonder if writers too look for a formula instead of a story, or band together for support in workshops; if book lovers begin to lose their eye and seize on any weak or fumbling or mundane story if only it has some germ of difference.

There is nothing new in a beginner's search for a formula. Every published writer is constantly asked for it, and feels guilty when all he can suggest is work.... It may be that each of us discovers, at some level, his own formula. What seems new to me is the broader conviction that nonwriters can be turned into writers by the application of some general formula, one that can be taught like a crochet stitch or a swimming stroke.... A workshop is a good thing for stimulating beginnings, and probably for working on film or video, where a number of writers may work on one story. Sitting in front of your television set in the attitude of a consumer, you can see how well it works.

But a story told in print is a lone and intense experience for the reader. Rationalized inconsistencies won't do; it needs the lone, intense, and single-minded drive of authorship. Even so, a workshop often helps a nervous beginner to stand alone, and supplies him with a useful crutch. What worries me is the thought of any writer accepting the crutch as a regular tool. The best use I can think of for a crutch is to beat about the head anyone who tries to lay a finger on my story.

Does all this really mean, as I sometimes fear, a new approach to the ancient skill of storytelling? A kind of mass production and mass consumption? If so, the writer with the secret vision, and the lonely need to turn it into a story, will not go away. He has withstood the belief that his craft was sinful, that it was a teaching aid, that it was outworn, that it had nothing to say; he will not blanch at learning that it should be assembled by a committee from prefabricated plastic parts. He will find some crazy, off-beat listener, in the mental homes if necessary, and go on telling stories in his own old way. Perhaps, in some dusty attic, he will even come across an old steam-driven typewriter, and bring out a copy or two. But he will miss the delight of a wider sharing; the magic will be gone.

And then, perhaps—if the caring community has survived and has not been stretched too thin—out of the branches may fall a great golden apple inscribed with the name of Hans Christian Andersen; and, bypassing all the plastic stories, it may tumble into his lap. And there will be magic again, and he will know that he is a lucky writer, and cherish his golden apple as I do.

References

Livingston, M.C. (1958). *Whispers and other poems*. Orlando, FL: Harcourt Brace Jovanovich.

Livingston, M.C. (1959). *Wide awake and other poems*. Orlando, FL: Harcourt Brace Jovanovich.

Livingston, M.C. (1962). *See what I found*. Orlando, FL: Harcourt Brace Jovanovich.

Livingston, M.C. (Ed.). (1968). *A tune beyond us: A collection of poems*. Orlando, FL: Harcourt Brace Jovanovich.

Livingston, M.C. (1969). *A crazy flight and other poems*. Orlando, FL: Harcourt Brace Jovanovich.

Livingston, M.C. (1973). *When you are alone/it keeps you Capone: An approach to creative writing*. New York: Atheneum.

Livingston, M.C. (1976). *4-way stop and other poems*. New York: Atheneum.

Livingston, M.C. (1980). *No way of knowing: Dallas poems*. New York: Atheneum.

Livingston, M.C. (1981). *The writing of poetry* (filmstrip series). Orlando, FL: Harcourt Brace Jovanovich Films.

Livingston, M.C. (1984). *The child as poet: Myth or reality?* Boston, MA: The Horn Book.

Livingston, M.C. (1985). *Worlds I know and other poems*. New York: Atheneum.

Livingston, M.C. (1990). *Climb into the bell tower: Essays on poetry*. New York: Harper & Row.

Roethke, T. (1986). *The collected poems of Theodore Roethke*. New York: Doubleday.

Wrightson, P. (1968). Hans Christian Andersen Award acceptance speech, in *Bookbird, 3-4*, 23-26. Vienna: International Institute for Children's Literature and Reading Research.

How to Write Books for Children and Young Adults

Ginny Moore Kruse

In this chapter, Kruse—director of the Cooperative Children's Book Center of the University of Wisconsin-Madison and an experienced teacher, librarian, and writer— presents specific information about preparing and submitting a children's book for publication. She opens with a discussion of the reasons for writing children's books. Then she reviews the resources available to authors. She notes the importance of reading current children's books and describes how to find out which books have been successful. The chapter concludes with an outline of the typical steps involved in submitting a manuscript for publication.

■ ■ ■ ■

So you want to write books for children. Teachers and other professionals who work with children or children's materials are often highly motivated to create their own books for several reasons. One motivation may be the children themselves. Seeing their responses to trade books can provide an abundance of original book ideas: "I could write like that," or "If only that story had been..." or "The things these children say and do every day would make such good stories." These are all valid motivations for writing a children's picture book, information book, novel, or biography.

Practical, professional knowledge of the dimensions of a successful children's book is important background for a potential author. So are firsthand awareness of some of the situational or ethical dilemmas of today's youth and knowledge of how to use trade books in a literature-based curriculum. However, this knowledge alone does not automatically transform an effective, observant teacher into a published writer of children's books. What, then, does prepare an unpublished writer to create books for children?

There is no single checklist to complete, conference to attend, course to take, how-to book to buy, or formula to follow for getting a children's book published. Most authors and publishers in this field agree on several points, however. One is that it is important to know why you want to write children's books. Writing is hard work, full of discouragements as well as satisfactions. Most children's authors cannot support themselves on the income derived from their books. Writing under these circumstances requires dedication. Another truism is that in order to write well when either the time to write is available or the inspiration strikes, a writer must be in practice. Most writers write regularly, just as runners prepare for races and pianists practice for concerts. Madeleine L'Engle says writers must be "ready to serve the gift."

If after reading this chapter you decide that writing children's books for publication may not be what you are called to do after all, be honest with yourself. Perhaps you would prefer to share copies of the stories you've written with family members and close friends by using desktop publishing and community printing resources rather than by submitting them to a trade book publisher that receives several thousand unsolicited manuscripts annually.

Children's book publisher Norma Jean Sawicki once asked participants at a conference of the Midwest Society of Children's Book Writers why they wanted to write for publication. She pointed out that not all runners compete in the Boston Marathon, but they still enjoy running regularly, and some of them are extremely good at what they do. Not all pianists, she continued, aspire to play in Carnegie Hall, but they gain great satisfaction from playing in their homes or at gatherings of friends and family members. Examining one's motivation is an essential first step for a writer.

Examining one's motivation is an essential first step for a writer. ■ ■ ■

Finding Out About Book Publishing

Every week at least one published or unpublished book creator uses the resources of the Cooperative Children's Book Center (CCBC). I notice some of the ways they prepare for what they do, and sometimes I can suggest more efficient and effective ways to prepare for sharing their writing with children or young teenagers.

First of all, I always suggest that they read the concise pamphlet "Writing Books for Children and Young Adults," published by the Children's Book Council (CBC). It is available for US50¢ plus a self-addressed, stamped envelope from the Order Center, Children's Book Council, 350 Scotland Rd., Orange, NJ 17050, USA. This compact flier contains the information a writer needs to know to write a letter of inquiry, prepare a manuscript for submission, and become involved in writing for children.

The next publication I recommend is *Writing Books for Young People*, an outstanding manual by James Giblin (1990). This book is full of straightforward, practical, accurate information about preparing to write, writing different kinds of children's books, contacting publishers, submitting manuscripts, obtaining a copyright, and other important procedures. The book is available at the public library, but since you cannot keep it checked out forever, order your own copy from a local bookstore.

Some people recommend sending for publishers' seasonal book catalogs to get a good idea of their publishing programs. I think this is a waste of time. Getting such catalogs can only serve to dazzle, distract, or even discourage you by making you wonder if there is any place for your book idea. In any case, most publishers are well into the next year's publishing program by the time their current catalog goes into the mail, so you are operating with less than up-to-date information.

However, it is worthwhile attending one of the large national conferences at which trade book publishers are exhibiting so you actually can examine the newest children's books. The best conferences for this type of hands-on examination are the American Booksellers Association (ABA) convention and the American Library Association (ALA) conference. Each organization meets annually, and these conference exhibits afford unusually fine opportunities to examine books. Both organizations schedule their conferences years in advance, so write to them for information about their meeting dates and sites, or look for this information in such publications as *American Libraries* and *Publishers Weekly*, available at most public libraries.

The CBC offers an annual listing of members' publishing programs with a succinct description of each. Send a self-addressed, stamped envelope to the CBC at the address noted previously requesting a copy of their "Members Publishing Programs" pamphlet. Once this listing arrives, look at it carefully and mark the publishers whose programs seem to fit your talents and interests. Go to the public library, a bookstore, or one of the national conferences and examine the books of the publishers whose focus most closely matches your own book idea.

The CBC's New York City office houses a collection of books by member publishers that can be examined with advance arrangements; write to the CBC at 568 Broadway, Suite 404, New York, NY 10012, USA for details.

The best source of up-to-date information about the children's book industry is the *Bulletin* of the Society of Children's Book Writers (SCBW). This bimonthly newsletter is devoted to the writing and publishing of children's books and was developed for use by active writers. It is more than worth the annual SCBW membership fee, which in 1991 is US$35. The *Bulletin* carries information about new children's book editors and publishers' needs, as well as reviews of books of interest to professional book authors, announcements of new publications and upcoming conferences, and writing tips. Reading the *Bulletin* on a regular basis is far more valuable than subscribing to standard writers' magazines such as *Writer's Market* and *The Writer*, which you can scan at the public library.

Membership in SCBW is open to anyone, and manuscript critiquing services are available by mail within the membership. An annual listing of children's book markets, agents, book packagers, and other helpful material is available to SCBW members for return postage. The SCBW address is PO Box 66296, Los Angeles, CA 90066, USA.

Writers who are also artists should locate the outstanding book *Writing with Pictures: How to Write and Illustrate Children's Books* (Shulevitz, 1985). This book is an unparalleled exploration of the creation of effective visual and written images. It also offers the generous insights of an award-winning book creator. (By the way, Shulevitz's summer institutes are worth the expense and time for artists interested in creating picture books.)

Writers who are not artists should refrain from engaging an illustrator for their unpublished manuscripts. Book publishers prefer to match a manuscript with an illustrator themselves, often pairing a known illustrator with a new writer, or sometimes vice versa. Writers who submit manuscripts with art by someone else will likely receive a rejection slip because of the artistic and business considerations involved.

Some of the most exciting developments in U.S. children's book publishing happen at the regional level or through special interest publishers. Most of these smaller publishers cannot meet the CBC's membership requirements because of the small number of books they publish each year. However, two reliable sources of information about small publishers exist. One is the *Directory of Alternative Press Publishers of Children's Books* (Horning, 1991), published through the CCBC and available from the Friends of the CCBC, PO Box 5288, Madison, WI 53705, USA. Although this directory was not created for use by writers (its main purpose is to help people secure children's books published by small presses), it is the only resource devoted solely to providing information about low-volume children's book publishers.

The other information source is the National Minority Publishers Exchange *Newsletter*, which provides information about minority authors, illustrators, and publishers. To get information about the resources and services available from this national coalition, write to Charles Taylor, c/o Praxis Publications, 2215 Atwood Ave., Madison, WI 53704, USA.

A word about institutes and courses is in order. Reliable children's book publishing institutes are offered annually at campuses such as Vassar and Radcliffe. As outstanding as they are, the emphasis of these institutes is on becoming involved in publishing, not on writing books. In contrast, many campuses across the country offer occasional writing workshops or academic courses on writing for children. These are worthwhile opportunities for people who need an instructor's direct feedback on their writing. When inquiring, ask to be put in touch with two or three people who took the course the last time it was offered so you can evaluate how worthwhile it might be.

Correspondence courses on writing for children are advertised widely in newspapers and magazines. These courses may be worth the expense to a person who needs both discipline and written feedback. Those interested in a correspondence course should explore the backgrounds of the faculty and request an instructor whose published work is similar to the type of writing they are interested in. Keep in mind, however, that one can purchase various writing guides, attend one or more conferences, and even enroll in a summer writers' workshop for the amount of money invested in a correspondence course.

Finding Out About Current Children's Books

One of the first steps recommended in both the CBC pamphlet and the Giblin (1990) manual is one that many people are unwilling to take the time to complete: read newly published books written for children and young adults. This is one of the keys to getting published, and it's easy to do. Many erstwhile authors are so intent on writing children's books as they remember them to be that they neglect to read the books being published today—the books currently considered to be successful in the field. In their haste to begin writing, they overlook an important investment in themselves as writers. I encourage writers to examine books in public libraries, school libraries, and good, independently owned children's book stores.

Further, I recommend asking a school or public librarian which books have remained popular during the past 5 to 10 years. Read some of these books and try to determine what makes them successful. In addition, ask to see some of the outstanding books published in the past year. For instance, look at the books selected most recently as "Children's Choices" or "Teachers' Choices" (listed annually in *The Reading Teacher*), or as "Young Adults' Choices" (listed annually in the *Journal of Reading*). (These annotated lists are available separately from the International Reading Association.) Also look at the books listed by the

American Library Association as "Notable Children's Books" or "Best Books for Young Adults" (listed annually in *Booklist* and also available separately from ALA). These books are admired by children and young adults or by professionals who work closely with young readers and who know the new books well.

Even if you are currently teaching, it's important for you to gain an up-to-date sense of the children's book field from a writer's perspective. The books you know from your college course on children's literature or the ones you use in your classroom and school on a regular basis are only a few of the tens of thousands of books in print for children in the United States. Although it's not necessary to enroll in another children's literature course, and you certainly do not need to read thousands of children's books in order to work seriously on your own writing, it is essential to get an idea of what is being published and where your book ideas may fit in. Although some writers may feel hindered from developing original ideas after reading books written by others, most are convinced that knowing what kinds of books are being published is the best way to equip themselves to create viable new books for today's children.

As director of the CCBC, a noncirculating research library and book examination center of contemporary and historical children's and young adult literature, I have the opportunity to see most of the trade books for young readers published in the United States each year. The number in 1990 was close to 5,000. At the CCBC, we see the hardcover and paperback books originating from the 60 or so CBC member publishers. We also see the growing number of children's books published by small, independently owned book publishers.

Each year we see new books for babies and for beginning readers. We see books for children who love to read and for those for whom reading is hard work. The new books each year include short and long novels for all age groups, original poetry and poetry anthologies, joke books and activity books, biographies, concept books, books about the natural world, and books about contemporary issues. You name it, and a book has probably been published about it. However, the book may not have been successful for any number of literary, artistic, financial, or other reasons; either way, your idea may still be a valid one.

The books I have been describing are not written expressly for instructional purposes, even though some of them may form the core of a literature-based curriculum. They are the books teachers and parents alike choose to read out loud to children for the sheer joy of hearing words put together well, for the fun of a good story, or for the community that grows in a classroom or household when a story is shared.

These are the types of books people belonging to the SCBW and attending one of the many writers' workshops around the country are hoping to write for publication. These are the books reviewed in journals such as *The Reading Teacher*, the *Journal of Reading, Language Arts, The New Advocate, Book Links, School Library Journal, The Horn Book, The Bulletin of the Center for Children's Books, The Web, The Voice of Youth Advocates, Kirkus, Publishers Weekly, Social Studies and the Young Learner*, and *Appraisal*. You can find most of these journals, plus others, at your school library/media center or your public library.

You do not need to read these journals regularly to write books for children, but they can give you some guidance about qualities to strive for and pitfalls to avoid. Also, your published book will need to receive good reviews in these journals to catch the attention of teachers and librarians, who are the key to introducing new books to children and young adults. Some books receive so much advance promotion that bookstores across the country stock them. For a beginning writer, such promotion is unlikely, however; a good review can be valuable, spurring librarians and teachers to buy your book and possibly prompting your publisher to accept a second and third manuscript.

Submitting Your Manuscript for Publication

Although the information resources listed previously contain extensive guidelines for submitting a manuscript, I will briefly summarize the steps most broadly accepted as standard in the field.

After you have written, revised, and rewritten several drafts of your manuscript, you may feel ready to describe your book to a publisher. Compose a letter of inquiry outlining what your book is about and explaining what makes it unique, important, and timely. Do not send query letters before you have completed the manuscript because your book will change as you create it, sometimes substantially. Avoid advising a potential publisher about editorial matters such as the exact audience for your book, who should illustrate the book, or the appearance of the book jacket. Leave these details up to the publisher.

Publishing is a business, so give your manuscript and all correspondence a professional, businesslike appearance. Type all your correspondence as business letters; do not use personal correspondence paper or hand write your letter. Proofread your letter carefully, and print it using a letter-quality printer.

Based on your earlier research, you will have decided which publishers to whom you will send query letters. If more than a year has elapsed since you obtained a listing of publishers, send for another or check the *Literacy Market Place* (updated annually) to make certain you are writing to the current editors at their correct addresses.

It's fine to send query letters simultaneously to several publishers. Retain copies of your letters and keep a separate query list with dates on file for quick referral. Enclose a self-addressed, stamped business envelope with each query letter. Do *not* send your manuscript along with your query letter. Wait for an editor to request that it be sent. The only exception to this rule is when your manuscript is extremely short—for example, the text of a 32-page picture book. Then you may choose to enclose the actual manuscript with the query letter.

If you submit your manuscript to more than one publisher simultaneously, you absolutely *must* inform each publisher of this. Complex business and even legal problems can develop if you do not indicate multiple submissions from the beginning. Furthermore, you run a great risk of damaging your reputation as a writer.

It is not necessary to copyright your manuscript before sending it to a publisher. You will have a copy of your manuscript and dated correspondence to demonstrate that the idea and manuscript are yours. See Giblin (1990) for details on copyrighting.

Print your manuscript with a letter-quality printer on standard-size paper. Include a running head (your name) and page number on each page of the manuscript. Send only good, clean photocopies of your manuscript to a publisher. Retain the original for your records. Enclose a self-addressed stamped mailer of the appropriate size so the publisher can return your manuscript if necessary. If you are submitting your manuscript after receiving a favorable response to a query letter, enclose a brief cover letter citing the earlier correspondence.

If you do not receive a response to your query letter within 6 weeks, send a brief follow-up letter, enclosing a copy of your original query. If you do not receive any response after another 6 weeks, you should move on; you do not want to be associated with a publisher whose office cannot handle editorial business in a reasonable time.

Always plan exactly to which editor and publisher you will send the next query letter or manuscript. Keep a dated record of all correspondence. If you send out multiple query letters, you may find one publisher asking you to submit your manuscript after you have already forwarded it to another. If this happens, explain the situation to the second publisher and tell them you'll keep them informed of the status and availability of your manuscript. Send your manuscript to this publisher next if it is rejected by the first publisher.

Allow publishers 3 months to review a full manuscript. If you have received no response after that amount of time, it is all right to write and inquire about the status of your manuscript. Refer to Giblin (1990) for additional advice about handling this delicate, nerve-wracking dimension of manuscript submission.

What should you do while your query letters or manuscripts are being considered by one or more publishers? Work on another manuscript, of course! Begin a new writing project, or work on revisions of another manuscript if a publisher has suggested this. Keep busy.

The business aspects of children's book writing and publishing are very clear to publishers and equally unclear to unpublished writers of children's books. Someone once referred to children's book writing as one of the last cottage industries, in that writers talk with one another infrequently about business matters, especially financial considerations. Unless writers belong to SCBW or have qualified to join the Authors' Guild (you are not ready to think about that at this stage), they may have little knowledge of the business end of the industry. Further, their motivation to be published may be so great that they do not pay close attention to these matters.

Occasionally writers will hear that securing an agent is important to becoming published. Most unpublished writers, however, will not benefit greatly from having an agent; they may not even be able to secure one. If you believe an agent will help in your situation, consult SCBW for information.

What if your manuscript is accepted? This is outstanding news, but recognize that more thinking and planning must be done. You will have to negotiate and sign a contract. The contract should specify subsidiary rights to your book, such as paperback or media adaptations, as well as the amount of money the publisher will send you after the contract is signed (your advance against royalties). If this is your first children's book, your advance is likely to be in the range of US$2,000-3,500. You will not receive more money until after the royalties from the sales of your published book exceed the amount of your advance.

A publisher may offer you a flat fee for your manuscript rather than a royalty arrangement (a percentage of all sales). Some very good writers and illustrators began their careers with flat fee arrangements. For example, many years ago Ellen Raskin received a flat fee of US$500 for her woodcuts illustrating Dylan Thomas's A *Child's Christmas in Wales*. Although the book is still reprinted, Raskin never realized any other income from it. However, the book brought her art to the attention of Jean Karl, then editor of Atheneum Children's Books. They worked together for years, during which time Raskin developed as a writer. She went on to receive the 1979 Newbery Award for *The Westing Game*. Similarly, Peter and Connie Roop signed *Keep the Lights Burning, Abbie* for a flat fee. After the book was adapted for television and shown on "Reading Rainbow," sales increased dramatically—as did the Roops' visibility and stature as children's book authors.

In spite of these generally happy flat fee stories, I usually advise against accepting such an arrangement. I make this recommendation because I've heard many other sorry personal narratives of authors who received little money for their works and lost virtually all control over them once the manuscript was sold. Refer to Giblin (1990) for details concerning a variety of contractual issues.

Writers often ask about manuscript reading groups—places to try out the text of a picture book or the opening chapter of a novel by reading it to children or adults. The experiences and opinions of published writers seem to vary considerably on the value of such feedback (see Livingston's comments in the preceding chapter). Certainly information books and novels set in a time and place other than those you have directly experienced should be read for accuracy and authenticity by someone who knows about these matters. Regarding the shape and style of your creative output, you will get as many opinions as you seek. People who know you will not be able to give you the objective, professional feedback you want and need. Therefore, presubmission reviews may not be helpful.

Hard Work But Significant Dividends

A number of years ago, 19-year-old Kevin Henkes walked into an appointment at Greenwillow Books and walked out with the promise of a contract for his first published children's book, *All Alone*. The story circulated within the writing community and even within the publishing industry about the young, completely unknown artist/author whose book was accepted the same day he showed it to a publisher.

This story is true. To say that it is unusual is an understatement, however. The portion of this overnight success story unknown to most people is that Henkes spent a full year reading contemporary children's books and examining those with successful designs and illustrations; finding out as much as he could about bookmaking and book production; researching what each publisher's books looked like in terms of his illustration style and writing interests; taking university courses in children's literature (it was during such a course that he developed the book); putting together a portfolio of artwork as well as the manuscript and art for *All Alone*; and writing for appointments with the publishers he wanted to see during a visit to New York City that he arranged at his own expense. In short, he invested a year's work to prepare for the day that launched what became a successful career of writing novels as well as writing and illustrating picture books for children.

As you see, success rarely, if ever, happens overnight. Rejection slips are typical. Almost all of the best and most successful writers in the field who were not already connected to the publishing industry through employment, friendship, or family ties went through many submissions, rejections, and discouragements before achieving their goal. Many of them tell their stories in one of two series of books on children's and young adult authors, *Something About the Author* (various editors, 1971-1991) and *Something About the Author: Autobiographical Series* (various editors, 1985-1991). It's important to expect rejection and not be discouraged by it. On the other hand, with a combination of solid preparation, talent, persistence, and a bit of luck, your manuscript may be accepted for publication.

As you strive toward the goal of getting published, it is important to remember that you have a built-in support network. Your young relatives and other family members will likely hang on every word you write, as will your friends and colleagues. They will rejoice with you when you sign a contract, celebrate each step that brings your manuscript closer to becoming a published book, and burst with happiness for you when the first bound copy is delivered. They will sustain you when a published review isn't as laudatory as they know your book deserves; they will line up for autographs when your local bookstore arranges for you to make an author appearance; they will send you copies of newspaper articles about your success; and they will invite you to speak at local events about being a published author. Your friends, colleagues, and family will be there with you and for you throughout your writing career. And so, everyone hopes, will the most important people of all: the young readers!

References

Giblin, J.C. (1990). *Writing books for young people.* Boston, MA: Writer, Inc.
Horning, K.T. (1991). *Directory of alternative press publishers of children's books* (4th ed.). Madison, WI: Cooperative Children's Book Center.
Literary market place. (annually). New York: R.R. Bowker.
Shulevitz, U. (1985). *Writing with pictures: How to write and illustrate children's books.* New York: Watson-Guptill.
Various editors. (1971-1991). *Something about the author* (Vols. 1-63). Detroit, MI: Gale Research.
Various editors. (1985-1991). *Something about the author: Autobiographical series.* (Vols. 1-11). Detroit, MI: Gale Research.

CHAPTER NINE

Developing Reading Programs: The Author's Role

John J. Pikulski

In this chapter, Pikulski describes the tasks and responsibilities involved in developing a reading series for publication. He begins with some historical background about writing reading programs before describing his experiences as a long-time member of the authorship team for the Houghton Mifflin reading/ language arts programs. He then describes the phases he has identified in developing and publishing reading programs, which include selecting authors; gathering background information; planning, writing, and editing the program; and evaluating the completed project.

■ ■ ■ ■

Publishing typically brings with it a prestige and respect that seem specially reserved for anything associated with the printed word. The term *author* seems to connote to most people a degree of respect, even awe. However, as one enters academia, where published authors are common, it becomes abundantly clear that not all publications are viewed as equally prestigious, scholarly, or worthwhile. For example, I recently heard a colleague ridicule a candidate for a faculty position because that candidate's vita included, under publications, an article entitled "The Overhead Projector Revisited." Similarly, many university administrators and promotion and tenure committees seem to consider textbook writing a contribution to teaching, or perhaps service, but not to scholarship.

Where does the writing of a developmental reading program fit on the continuum of prestige and scholarship? Probably not nearly as high as those of us associated with such authorship would like. Perhaps the problem began with McGuffey, whom many consider the father of modern published reading systems. Venezky (1987) reports that the McGuffey Eclectic Readers were:

> not markedly different from other readers of the time, their success coming from shrewd marketing practices rather than noteworthy content or pedagogy. In fact, McGuffey made his readers so much like his competitors' that he and his publisher were sued in 1838 for plagiarism by the publishers and author of the *Worcester Readers....* McGuffey and his publisher settled out of court for $2,000 and revised their readers immediately. However, some modern writers suggest that both Worcester and McGuffey borrowed liberally from a common source (p. 251).

It may be that early authors of basal readers, such as McGuffey and Worcester, condemned authors of reading programs to a rather ignominious beginning.

Integrity in Reading Programs

It would be naive to pretend that reading program authors are not the focus of a great deal of suspicion—suspicion that they sell their souls and their intellectual integrity in exchange for a yearly retainer or a royalty check. Indeed, one of the terms making the rounds at meetings of professionals in reading is *basal bashing*, which refers to a speech, article, or meeting in which reading programs and their authors are denounced as responsible for virtually all problems that exist in reading achievement.

While a confession on my part of an intellectual sellout might make this a more interesting chapter, my experiences with a publisher of a reading program have been professional, intellectually stimulating, and cordial (although the publisher has not always incorporated all of my suggestions into a particular program). Marketing considerations affect some decisions about reading programs, but I know of no such decision made when there was evidence to suggest that it would in any way interfere with a child's progress in learning to read. I am firmly convinced that virtually all major publishers of modern reading programs want to publish the best program possible. These publishers know that the best way to sell books is to produce materials that are highly effective in teaching children to read. Successful publishers would not incorporate a pedagogically unsound practice into their materials even if there were a marketing cry to do so—if for no other reason than that they recognize the long-term marketing folly of such a decision.

As an author, I have published journal articles, minor curriculum materials, and textbooks. Being a reading program author, however, is a very different experience from any of these other ventures. To begin with, publishing a developmental program that spans kindergarten to grade 8 is a much larger undertaking than almost any other school publishing effort. In my other publishing experiences, I have collaborated with no more than two other authors; the last major revision of a published reading program on which I worked had a team of 17 authors. On other types of projects, I have generally worked with one or two editors who have outlined any needed revisions and made minor editorial changes. On that last reading program revision, the editorial team consisted of 35 full-time editors, a sizable art department, technical consultants, and other contributors; the total number of people involved in producing the program exceeded 100.

It is important to keep in mind when reading this chapter that I am focusing on the authors' role in developing a reading program; therefore, the roles played by other professionals, such as editors, are not fully described. (The following chapter expands on these areas.) I do want to point out, however, that many of the reading program editors with whom I've worked have strong professional backgrounds that provide them with a great deal of insight into what will make an effective reading program. At the publisher I work with, most of the editors in the reading department have degrees in education, most have classroom teaching experience, and several hold doctorates and have published in scholarly journals. In my experience, the authors of published reading programs have enormous respect for the professional capability and contributions of the editors. Editors of published reading programs do far more than copyedit; they are highly creative professionals who contribute many important, innovative ideas to the development of the reading program. My contacts with reading program editors have been among the most professionally rewarding experiences I have had. The distinction between authors and editors in the development of a reading program is not nearly as distinct as the different titles imply.

The Author's Role

Building a reading program with the necessary array of materials needed to span from kindergarten to eighth grade is a gigantic, enormously complex task. The role the authors play in this construction varies from publisher to publisher. I recall a professional acquaintance some years ago telling me that he was about to sign a contract with a reading program publisher as an author, having made it very clear that he did not want to do any writing. The publisher had agreed to his terms and reportedly had planned for a group of freelance writers to produce that edition of the program. What this publisher apparently wanted was a "reading professional" with some degree of prominence listed among the authors to serve as a spokesperson for the program.

This story is echoed in Goodman et al.'s (1988) negative commentary on published reading programs, *Report Card on Basal Readers*. That report quotes a publisher's representative as responding in this way to the question of how senior authors of a basal are chosen: "That is a very premature question, if you are really interested in what makes this business tick. Author selection is one of the least important parts of putting together a series" (p. 55). Goodman et al. go on to point out that "this is not to say that authors are not knowledgeable, recognized authorities in the field" (p. 55). They also note that "how much actual writing the authors will do is variable from series to series and even within authorship teams" (p. 56).

The Goodman et al. report is based on limited, idiosyncratic reporting and presents a highly exaggerated, negative picture of what happens in the publishing of a reading series. (See Squire, 1987, for a response to the report.) However, it would be naive to suggest that no variability exists among authorship teams and publishers in the amount of responsibility authors have for producing reading programs.

In my experience, though, the vast majority of reading program authors are extraordinarily ethical and vitally concerned about improving the status of reading instruction and the quality of reading materials. Indeed, reading program authors, based on the full range of their professional contributions, are among the most prominent, most respected members of the reading profession. Certainly many publishers of reading programs require considerable writing, planning, and other contributions from their authors. In the work I have done with one reading series publisher, the amount of required writing has been considerable and has spanned virtually all phases of development.

The remaining sections of this chapter are devoted to describing an author's role in what I have judged to be the 10 phases of building a published reading program: (1) selecting the authors; (2) gathering background information; (3) checking applicability and workability of new ideas; (4) selecting literature for pupil texts; (5) planning the program's major dimensions; (6) developing specific plans, models, and outlines; (7) writing the program; (8) reviewing and editing the material; (9) selling the program; and (10) evaluating the published program.

The practices described in these phases are based largely on my experiences with one publisher. I did search the literature to find what others have written about publishing reading programs, but I found virtually nothing. Thus, these descriptions may be idiosyncratic and not at all representative of the experiences of other authors. In attempting to present an accurate and fair description of an author's role in publishing a developmental reading program, I have deliberately omitted a few details that seem unique (in a positive way) to the publisher with whom I am associated.

Phase 1: Selecting the Authors

Choosing the authors may be the most variable and most difficult to describe phase of developing a reading program, but it is a critically important one. It is also the phase that many people find the most interesting. Often people ask me how reading program authors are selected. Some seem to ask because of an interest in becoming authors; others ask just because they are curious.

The best generalization I can suggest is that reading educators are invited to become authors because they have made or are making some contribution to the profession that a publisher happens to admire. I have never seen, nor do I expect to see, an advertisement in the *Chronicle of Higher Education* for a reading program author; and frankly, I don't know of anyone who became an author because he or she wrote to a publisher expressing an interest in the job. My strong impression is that most major publishers of reading programs are constantly reading journals and attending conferences, and that one of the purposes they keep in mind during such professional activities is to identify potential new authors.

Some of the things publishers seem to look for in potential authors are professional prominence; the ability to conduct research (or a broad knowledge of research); practical experience in teaching reading; the ability to write clearly; creativity in approaching problems in the teaching of reading; expertise in a particular aspect of the teaching of reading, such as knowledge of children's literature, literacy education for children with limited English proficiency, assessment of reading, or the instruction of gifted or disabled readers; and effectiveness as a professional speaker. I am sure this list could be extended considerably. However, a publisher needs to construct a *team* of people whose professional activities and expertise complement each other. That is, they must be able to bring together a group of authors who have expertise in all major areas of concern in building a reading program.

One question that arises regarding the selection of authors is whether publishers feel the need to create a team that reflects a balance of geographic areas, cultures, races, and sexes. Certainly attention is given to such factors; however, in my experience, the primary consideration in choosing authors has been putting together a team that has wide-ranging experience in the various aspects of reading and that is familiar with the specific concerns of particular geographic regions and among various cultural or socioeconomic groups. When these considerations are foremost, a well-balanced group of authors emerges.

It is also important to note that, because of the scope of the task of publishing a reading program, authors can take on a variety of roles. Some senior-level authors have responsibility for virtually all aspects of the program. Other authors may work primarily on particular levels, such as the elementary grades. Still others may be asked to work with specific aspects of the program, such as designing activities for students with special needs or integrating writing activities with the reading selections.

Because of the scope of the task of publishing a reading program, authors can take on a variety of roles. ■ ■ ■

Phase 2: Gathering Background Information

In my experience, major revisions of reading programs occur on a 5-year cycle. In a major revision, most of the program's components (e.g., literature anthologies, teachers' guides, pupil response books) change dramatically. It is largely this type of revision that I will be discussing in the pages that follow. Minor revisions—which occur between major editions and involve such changes as adding new activities or altering the lessons in the teachers' guides—are often taken care of by the editorial staff after consultation with senior members of the authorship team.

Given the complexity of reading programs, a major revision requires several years of development. In my experience, the formal beginnings of a major reading program revision start with a review of published research and discussions with prominent researchers. In this phase, authors are expected to play the predominant role. While publishers and editors are far more familiar with research (and researchers) than I had ever imagined, the expectation is that the authors—many of whom are university based, and who themselves often produce journal articles and research reports—will be primarily responsible for keeping up to date with research and theory.

Even a full team of authors, however, will not have exper-tise in all the areas of research that might have implications for a new or revised reading program. In addition, there is a substan-tial time lag between conducting the research and publishing the results in professional journals. To compensate for this lag, the publisher I work with always has encouraged (and paid for) its authors to meet with other prominent, cutting-edge research-ers to discuss current research and its potential implications for reading instruction.

Reading program authors are expected to identify innova-tive researchers whose work might have implications for pro-gram development. In some cases, the research appears rather distant from practical application; thus, another major role of the authorship team is to translate experimental and theoretical research into more practical terms.

Critics of published developmental reading programs of-ten imply that publishers ignore or even suppress the results of research. My experience has been quite the contrary. My pub-lisher has made every conceivable effort to make use of the re-search conducted by members of its authorship team, to require a thorough review of available research, and to locate the most recent research findings by funding meetings with other cutting-edge researchers.

Phase 3: Checking Applicability and Workability

It is one thing for a group of researchers, authors, and edi-tors to become excited about recent research ideas; it is an-other thing to translate those ideas into something that teachers can use and that will indeed help children become better read-ers. Phase 3 of building a reading program begins shortly after the comprehensive research review and continues until produc-tion of the program begins. In a larger sense, it continues even when the program is available for use. This third phase involves determining whether authors and editors can present new ideas in a form that teachers and other reading educators will accept and use.

This checking of new ideas takes many forms. Discussions are held with respected practitioners and with the publisher's sales representatives and educational consultants. These company representatives are the people who have been selling and working to implement previous editions of the program; they often have enormously useful insights into what teachers find effective or troublesome about the current edition of a reading program. These representatives not only react to the authorship team's ideas but also make their own suggestions.

As ideas are translated into educational materials, they are sometimes tested in focus groups, a technique traditionally associated with consumer product sales. In a focus group, a small group of teachers may be shown several versions or interpretations of the same idea. They react to and discuss the materials while the publisher observes.

The role of authors in Phase 3 is quite variable, and only in preparing for this discussion did I seriously think about it. In my experience, authors and editors share about equally the job of judging the acceptability and applicability of suggested changes. Sometimes I've sensed an underlying, unspoken expectation that authors will aggressively promote change while editors will urge caution about departing radically from the current program, especially if that program has been successful. However, I've also been part of situations where editorial personnel have been the driving force in making dramatic changes.

Phase 4: Selecting Literature for Pupil Texts

The search for quality children's literature is an ongoing activity for publishers of reading programs. The publishing house with which I've worked employs full-time librarians to monitor children's books. These librarians are also responsible for surveying children's librarians to (1) determine the most popular books, and (2) identify books that may not yet have achieved widespread popularity but that seem to have considerable appeal for children.

Every effort is made to locate books of high literary merit as well as widespread appeal among children. Catalogs of award-winning books are consulted, along with annotated lists such as the International Reading Association's "Children's Choices" and "Young Adults' Choices," published annually. In addition, the publisher arranges for interviews with children who are asked to read and respond to books and selections.

Wherever possible, the publisher uses unedited, unabridged literature. Adaptations are kept to a minimum to preserve the literary integrity of the selection. However, potentially offensive language, references to characters or incidents that are meaningful in a full work but not in an excerpt chosen for the program, or unclear references occasionally require minor changes. In earlier editions of reading programs, at a time when readability formulae seemed almost universally accepted, there was substantial pressure to modify vocabulary and sentence length to satisfy these formulae. Thankfully, such pressure recently has decreased dramatically; in fact, my judgment is that today users of reading programs demand *no* adaptation of extant literature. Critics who still charge that reading programs massively distort published children's literature have not taken the time to look at the most recent editions from most major publishers.

In Phase 4, as in most others, authors have varying degrees of involvement. The children's literature experts on the team obviously have the highest degree of involvement and responsibility. They help locate books and authors, read and review books and other texts located by the publisher's librarians, and consult with teachers and children about their favorite books. Program authors also read all potential selections to determine their suitability in terms of social/psychological merit and conceptual reading challenge for a given level. They do not, however, write the main reading selections in the students' anthologies. And while program authors have considerable input in choosing literature for inclusion, the publisher provides a great deal of support in locating materials and assumes total responsibility for negotiating permission to use the works.

Phase 5: Planning the Program's Major Dimensions

Major plans for the program are developed at large meetings of authors, editors, and occasionally management. Some broad areas likely to be discussed include the following:

- Identifying content and materials that might become part of the program.
- Establishing the major outcomes or goals for the program.
- Determining ways in which the program will foster positive attitudes and habits in literacy.
- Establishing a plan for teaching decoding, comprehension, and other reading strategies.
- Ensuring that the program offers valid suggestions for integrating the language arts.
- Determining a general plan for presenting literature experiences and other instructional activities.
- Establishing an assessment plan for the program.

This tends to be an exciting stage in developing the reading program. At this point in planning, virtually all aspects of the previous edition of the program may be modified.

In Phase 5, the roles of various authors begin to be defined more clearly. In addition to deciding broadly what the new program will look like, the group settles on who will do what and when. It may also be decided that additional authors need to be added to the team. For example, if psycholinguistics is being touted as an important related discipline for understanding the reading process, the publisher may decide to add a psycholinguist to the team.

Overall, the goal of this phase is to develop the first working blueprints for the program's development. Authors play a lead role in these discussions. Sometimes the entire authorship team meets; at other times the team may break into two or three subgroups, each of which concerns itself with a different set of issues or with particular program levels.

Phase 6: Developing Specific Plans, Models, and Outlines

From an author's point of view, this may be the longest, most time-consuming phase in developing a reading program. In this stage, plans might be developed for the outcomes and strategies of each level of the program. Recent reading programs have centered around a literature unit. Decisions need to be made as to what selections will be included in each unit and in which order they will appear. In addition, decisions need to be made as to what, if anything, beyond literature selections will be included in pupil texts.

Models must be developed for strategy/skill lessons and for each component of the unit. This is a time when author-editor interaction is especially lively and productive. There are many revisions, with editors revising authors' work, authors revising what the editors return, and so forth. This high degree of give and take between authors and editors comes as a surprise to those who publish only journal articles or college texts, where the opportunities for ongoing contact between authors and editors tend to be more limited.

Phase 7: Writing the Program

All authors do some detailed writing, usually of teacher guide materials. Some authors prepare strategy lessons; others may write materials designed to extend students' understanding and appreciation of a literature selection. If pupil anthologies are to include content other than literature selections, the authors are usually responsible for preparing it. Because of the large volume of written materials, authors are sometimes assigned to write materials for only several levels of the program. Editors often share in some of the detailed writing, particularly of teacher guide materials.

The amount of detailed writing an author does varies considerably from person to person. Some authors write less and concentrate on reviewing material prepared by other authors before it reaches the publisher. For example, in the last major revision on which I worked, I was responsible for writing a few teacher guide lessons for the earliest levels of the program, which served as models for other authors. Subsequently I wrote less of these materials and spent more time reviewing and commenting on the work of other authors. Throughout the development of the program, however, I remained responsible for writing some strategy lessons.

Phase 8: Authors Become Editors

As Phase 7 implies, a considerable number of people work on various components of the reading program. Supervising editors and some of the authors are responsible for ensuring that all the pieces of the program are compatible and complementary and for maintaining continuity from level to level. As noted previously, at least some authors are expected to review work written and edited by others. Part of the reason for this review is to achieve the continuity just mentioned; however, an equally important responsibility is to ensure that no substantive changes or instructional problems have cropped up.

Some authors are expected to read galleys—not for proof-reading, although comments here are always appreciated, but to ensure that nothing contradictory or pedagogically unsound has crept into the program in the final stage of editing.

Phase 9: Representing the Program

Once a program is written and published, the job of selling it remains. Obviously, major publishers have teams of managers, sales representatives, and consultants who are in charge of selling programs and helping schools implement them. In the 10 years I have been associated with a publisher of reading programs only once have I presented a program directly to educators who were considering purchasing it. That presentation was neither arranged nor sanctioned by the publisher; it was arranged, without my knowledge, by a zealous school administrator.

While I do not promote reading programs, I do make between 50 and 75 unrelated presentations a year that are sponsored by my publisher (other authors of reading programs may make far fewer presentations). Virtually all of these talks are at professional meetings. Often they are to various groups affiliated with the International Reading Association or to the faculties of school districts as part of their inservice programs. The publisher never controls the content of my presentation and does not expect me to speak about or even mention the reading program. I talk about topics such as comprehension strategies, how to implement a literature-based reading program, reading assessment, vocabulary development, and the implications of recent research. While I'm sure the publisher wants to support professional staff development in the spirit of altruism, I strongly suspect that management also hopes the goodwill generated by the company's sponsorship of my participation, as well as the heightened visibility of an author of their reading program, will have some indirect benefit in promoting the program.

Phase 10: Evaluating the Program

In the first year after a major program revision, I spend a great deal of time in one or two nearby schools that are using the new edition. I try to work with the principal, the reading specialist, and the teachers to build an understanding of the philosophy behind the materials. I also visit classrooms to teach reading using the program and meet regularly with teachers, both in groups and individually. I learn very quickly which aspects of the program are working well, and any problems are immediately brought to my attention. I become less involved with direct evaluation after the first year, but in traveling to many professional meetings and talking with teachers and administrators who are using the program—as well as with sales representatives and consultants—I continually reexamine the program.

Conclusion

Given the space limitations for this chapter, I've provided only the most global, general description of how a published developmental reading program is brought into being and the role an author plays in that process. Building a reading program is a costly, complicated project. Although there are those in our profession who perceive the authoring of such materials as unscholarly or even harmful to the educational well-being of students, published reading programs continue to be by far the most commonly used reading instructional materials in the United States. I can't think of many activities with more potential power for bringing about change and improvement in the teaching of reading than developing the best possible published reading programs.

In my experience, great care, much planning, and enormous resources and talent go into the building of a published reading program. Given the gigantic numbers of teachers and

Pikulski

students who are influenced by those readers, I will continue to count my authorship role in this process as being among my most important professional contributions. I can also say unequivocally that serving as an author of a major published reading program has been both challenging and intellectually stimulating. Writing such programs is approached, not only by the authors but by the editors and publisher as well, as a very serious and scholarly activity.

References

Goodman, K.S., Shannon, P., Freeman, Y.S., & Murphy, S. (1988). *Report card on basal readers*. Katonah, NY: Richard C. Owen.

Squire, J.R. (1987, November). A *publisher responds to the basal reader report card*. Paper presented at the meeting of the National Council of Teachers of English, Los Angeles, CA.

Venezky, R.L. (1987). A history of the American reading textbook. *Elementary School Journal, 87*, 247-265.

Publishing Reading and Language Arts Programs

Cynthia J. Orrell

In this chapter, Orrell discusses the contributions of authors in the planning, development, and marketing of a reading program. She then describes the roles of others involved in the publishing cycle, including editors, librarians, writers, marketing specialists, sales representatives, and service consultants. As an executive editor for reading with Silver Burdett & Ginn, Orrell gives an insider's view of the important qualifications for each of these roles. She concludes by offering specific suggestions for acquiring a position with a reading program publisher.

■ ■ ■ ■

Other chapters in this book provide tips on authoring journal articles, newspaper articles, professional books, children's trade books, supplementary instructional materials, and the like. However, discussing the authorship of a K-8 developmental reading/language arts program requires a slightly different point of view because with this type of project the author's position differs in several respects from the traditional role.

One difference is that a reading/language arts program is rarely, if ever, written by one author. It is a collaborative effort between the publisher and a group of 10 or more authors. Another difference is that programs take years rather than days or weeks to prepare, and the process seems endless—write, test, revise, retest, rewrite, and finally publish. In this chapter, I'll outline briefly the role authors assume in developing published reading/language arts programs. Then I'll focus on the roles that other contributors play in this process.

The Role of the Author

As I see it, the role of reading program authors is twofold. First, the authors help formulate a comprehensive program plan, using the latest research and classroom wisdom. The plan lays out the program's philosophy, describes components and major features, and includes sample units and lessons. Second, authors monitor program development for strict adherence to the standards of quality set forth in that plan.

As Pikulski notes in the previous chapter, the exact responsibilities of an author vary from publisher to publisher and from project to project. However, typical tasks in formulating a program plan include conducting research, reviewing the research of others, writing and trying out prototype lessons, and training the editorial staff in the pedagogy underlying the program. During program development, authors might select stories for the student texts, prepare their portions of the teaching materials, review materials written by others, and help fine-tune the program plan. Once the program is published, authors may train sales representatives and consultants in certain program features and answer questions from teachers and administrators.

Authors are the spirit of a reading program. Their collective vision shapes the program's philosophy. Their standards of quality are reflected in each component. In my experience, authors energize and encourage the rest of us when problems seem unresolvable, and they come through when deadlines loom.

Who Writes Reading Programs?

Authors of developmental reading programs form a small group—there are probably fewer than 100 in the United States. They certainly make up a small fraction of the total number of authors of the types discussed in this book.

Authors are the spirit of a reading program. Their collective vision shapes the program's philosophy. ■ ■ ■

Reading program authors are generally members of the academic community—professors or researchers in education—who have been selected by publishers for this role. Publishers choose authors to match a number of criteria. As Pikulski mentions, scholarship, research, overall contribution to the study of reading, and particular areas of expertise all come into play. Also important are an interest in translating research into practical, child- and teacher-centered curricula and compatibility with other authors selected for the project.

Another criterion publishers must consider is the time a potential author can devote to a project. Contrary to statements in the *Report Card on Basal Readers* (Goodman et al., 1988) that authors contribute little to a program beyond their names, my experience is that authors commit a great deal of time and effort in all phases of the publishing cycle, from planning through development and into marketing and sales.

Other Roles in Publishing Reading Programs

Although authorship opportunities in this field are few, there are many other ways to contribute to the development of a reading/language arts program. I'd like to describe some of the opportunities that exist and then suggest how educators might go about offering their talents to a publishing company.

Pikulski provides a complete description of 10 major stages of the publishing cycle, so I won't go into the details of each stage here. For reference, though, keep in mind three general steps in publishing a developmental reading program: (1) planning, (2) writing and producing the books, and (3) presenting the program to teachers and schools. Each step of the process requires the talents and efforts of many people.

Editors

Editors, like authors, are involved in the entire publication cycle. They help plan the program, and they monitor its development to ensure that each component adheres to the plan. In early stages, editors review research, evaluate other programs, and suggest instructional approaches. They talk with teachers, analyze published tests and district curricula, and gather any other information that might be useful in shaping basic pedagogy and instructional design. Once the program plan has been approved, editors help choose stories and poems for the students' textbooks. They evaluate the quality of the instructional materials—teacher editions, workbooks, charts, tests—and revise or rewrite them as needed. Editors conduct field tests, read copy, check page references, generate indexes, specify and approve art, and make sure the right cover gets on the right book.

Certainly, editorial work is varied. Some tasks require initiative and creativity; some require excruciating attention to detail. All require thorough knowledge of teachers, children, classrooms, and reading instruction. Although editors sometimes work in groups, much of the work is solitary—an editor, a stack of copy, and a deadline. Most editors come to the job with teaching experience and at the very least an undergraduate degree in education. Many have graduate degrees as well as previous editorial experience.

Librarians

Librarians are needed for two major roles: maintaining a publisher's reference library and recommending literature for inclusion in the series. Some publishing companies employ full-time children's and reference librarians, while others contract librarians for specific projects. Librarians might be asked to conduct surveys of students' reading preferences, negotiate with children's authors to write for the series, conduct editorial staff development sessions on children's literature, or recommend titles for specific grades.

One example project was Silver Burdett & Ginn's Reader's Choice Award, in which our regular panel of librarians ran a nationwide review of stories by children. The librarians helped organize the review and, for the early grades, read the stories to children. They evaluated the stories themselves and then helped the children prepare reviews. Selections that children voted as their favorites were given the Reader's Choice Award. In addition, the children's evaluations of story appeal and reading difficulty influenced our decisions about whether to include a story in the reading program and at what grade.

In general, librarians are most heavily involved in the early and middle stages of the publishing cycle, when the program plan is being prepared and the student materials are being developed. The most desirable candidate for a publisher's librarian would be a school librarian with a strong interest in education and research. Special expertise in minority literature is always in demand. In fact, there seems to be a new specialty for librarians: reviewing children's literature, particularly minority literature, in all content areas.

Freelance Writers

Because publishers generally want reading/language arts programs to be written, revised, edited, and published in as short a time as possible, they frequently contract with freelance educational writers during the middle stages of program development. Working from a detailed outline prepared by the program's editors and authors, these writers prepare first drafts of sections of a manual or workbook. The drafts (which are expected to conform in substance and format to samples provided by the publisher) are reviewed, edited, and rewritten until they match the program plan exactly.

Freelance program writers generally have either teaching backgrounds or previous experience with educational publishers. Thorough understanding of children and classrooms is a must, as are writing skills and attention to detail.

Marketing Specialists and Researchers

Many people assume that the sole role of the marketing department is to advertise and sell published materials. These are marketing functions but, in truth, marketing has many roles, including that of "the voice of the teacher" during program development. Since marketing specialists are in regular contact with schools and teachers, they are up to date on issues that teachers face.

In the early stages of program development, marketing specialists help determine the best date of publication to meet state and local textbook adoption deadlines. As sample materials are written, marketing specialists arrange for editorial field tests and pilot programs. They also conduct basic market research—surveying teachers and administrators, analyzing competitive materials, and conducting focus groups. Once a program is published, of course, marketing specialists are instrumental in launching it. They prepare exhibits for conventions, train sales representatives in program features, and develop advertisements and brochures.

An essential qualification for a marketing specialist in a textbook publishing company is experience and interest in education. Most of these marketing specialists have teaching backgrounds; many also have educational sales experience or degrees in business. The job involves travel, creativity, and skill in statistical analysis, writing, and public speaking.

Sales Representatives and Service Consultants

Sales representatives and service consultants are the publishing people best known to school personnel. They present programs to schools and help them implement the program once purchased. They advise on such matters as placement, grouping, and pacing when the program is first adopted and suggest variations and new approaches when a program has been in use for several years. Sales representatives also help develop selling strategies for an area and monitor accounts to ensure that the right materials are delivered on time and to the right place. Service consultants make presentations, prepare inservice materials, correlate published materials with district curricula, and work with teachers to resolve any concerns about the daily use of the program.

For either position, the ability to make presentations and think on your feet are crucial. Extensive travel is required. Service consultants have teaching experience or some prior affiliation with schools, and many have graduate degrees in education. Sales representatives also commonly have teaching backgrounds. For this position, previous direct sales experience is desirable.

Getting Your Foot in the Door

As you can see, there are many ways to be involved in publishing a reading program. If you're interested in such a career, here are a few tips.

Prepare your résumé and everything else you send with care—publishers do not overlook typographical errors, misspellings, or squeezed margins. Keep your communications short and to the point; a résumé over two pages is more likely to be thrown away than read. Explain in a cover letter the kind of position you are interested in and what skills and experiences you have to offer.

Experience is important. Describe any experience you have in teaching, curriculum development or review, textbook selection, and writing or editing. Membership in professional organizations such as the International Reading Association is important; so is experience with planning units of study and developing materials, even if for only one classroom. If you are interested in becoming a sales representative or consultant, be sure to include any background in public speaking or direct sales.

One way to get experience—and see whether publishing is for you—is to work on a freelance basis. Publishers often hire freelancers to fill in during a crunch, and editorial development houses rely on freelancers for their writing and editing contracts. A useful reference book for freelancers, or anyone interested in publishing, is *Literary Market Place* (updated annually). Available in most libraries, the book lists names, addresses, and phone numbers of publishers as well as the many firms that publishers contract with during the course of a project. Look for the managing editor and give him or her a call; these editors can tell you whether any departments need freelance help and will often suggest whom you might contact. And, according to my own managing editor, they are the people most likely to answer their phones.

Working on a reading/language arts program, whether as an editor, an author, or a sales representative, is challenging and exciting. It is an opportunity to provide teachers with the best possible materials for teaching children to read. It is a chance to understand American education from a national perspective and to work with some of the finest thinkers in the field. I hope the information I've been able to provide in this chapter is of help to those of you who would like to join in the effort.

References

Goodman, K.S., Shannon, P., Freeman, Y.S., & Murphy, S. (1988). *Report card on basal readers*. Katonah, NY: Richard C. Owen.

Literary market place. (updated annually). New York: R.R. Bowker.

C H A P T E R **E L E V E N**

Writing Supplemental Materials in Reading and Language Arts
Dale D. Johnson

In this chapter, Johnson discusses the process of authoring supplemental educational materials in reading and language arts. He describes various types of supplemental materials and their instructional purposes and outlines the kind of content that can be addressed in reading and language arts workbooks. A widely published author of supplemental materials, Johnson offers practical suggestions for securing a publisher. He also presents tips to help novice writers maintain the demanding writing schedule typically required for developing supplemental materials. He concludes with a discussion of the benefits of workbook authorship.

■ ■ ■ ■

If you are thinking about becoming an author of supplemental materials, get ready to thicken your skin! In recent years, "basal bashing" and "supplemental slamming" have become increasingly fashionable exercises among some regulars on the lecture circuit. Various professors, self-styled "language theorists," and assorted others who never knew or have long forgotten what it is like to teach elementary or secondary students all day every day seem to take great pleasure in finding and exhibiting examples of silly, unimportant, or poor-quality skill and drill activities. Catchy speech and article titles like "Dr. Ditto Died Today and No One Even Noticed" can be found in many conference programs and in the tables of contents of journals and magazines aimed at teachers. So if you decide to write supplementary materials, be prepared to become a target.

But despite this surge in vitriolic attacks by a vocal minority, the popularity of supplemental materials among teachers continues to increase each year. Why are supplements, which have been popular for 50 years, still in such great demand? What accounts for their widespread use? Simply speaking, supplemental materials have been so successful because they are based on a solid foundation of learning theory: humans learn by doing. When a teacher's goal is to help students appreciate quality literature, the students should read good literature. When a teacher's goal is to help students learn and use specific skills and strategies, the students should be provided with focused opportunities to practice those skills and strategies. Supplemental materials are designed to do just that. So if you want to author supplements, remember that for every armchair critic who attacks what you write, 100 teachers will show you they value what you've done by using your product in their classrooms.

Many different kinds of materials reside under the "supplement" umbrella. Everything from workbooks and ditto masters to teacher resource books and kits to ancillaries such as games, puppets, posters, audio and video cassettes, films and filmstrips, and computer softwear are referred to as supplements. They are designed to supplement the teacher's regular instructional program, whether it revolves around a reading or language arts basal series, collections of trade books and anthologies of literature, or "real life" materials like menus, manuals, and pamphlets. This chapter deals with only one category of supplements: workbooks that emphasize reading and writing (paper and pencil) activities.

Workbooks: Purposes and Design

Most workbook series are developed to achieve all or most of these four objectives:

- To provide instruction or review.
- To provide practice with what has been taught or reviewed.
- To help students apply the skills or strategy to other texts.
- To help students extend what has been learned, practiced, and applied.

Each workbook lesson is designed to focus on a specific skill or strategy with which the teacher decides his or her students need help. The example beginning on the next page, "Using Graphic Aids," is excerpted from a workbook series designed to improve intermediate grade students' use of study skills (*Reading in the Content Area*, Level F, 1989). The lesson illustrates one employment of the teach-practice-apply-extend format typical of reading and language arts workbooks. Some workbook lessons don't incorporate all four steps, but virtually all include at least the practice step.

Workbook Content

Workbooks lend themselves to skill and strategy development with just about any element of the reading/language arts curriculum, including the following:

- *Word identification*—phonics, contextual analysis, structural analysis
- *Vocabulary*—classification, analogy, multiple meanings, denotation/connotation, synonyms/antonyms, homophones/homographs, etymology, word play

Figure
Excerpt from a Study Skills Workbook

LESSON

2 Using Graphic Aids

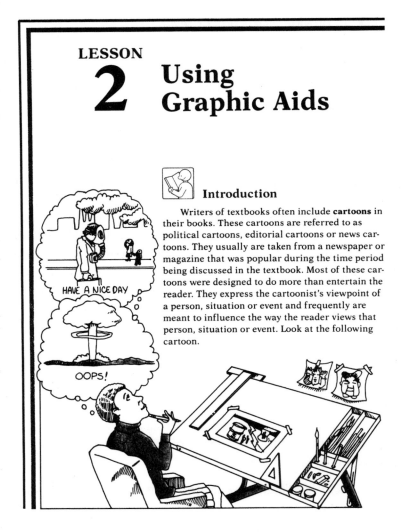

Introduction

Writers of textbooks often include **cartoons** in their books. These cartoons are referred to as political cartoons, editorial cartoons or news cartoons. They usually are taken from a newspaper or magazine that was popular during the time period being discussed in the textbook. Most of these cartoons were designed to do more than entertain the reader. They express the cartoonist's viewpoint of a person, situation or event and frequently are meant to influence the way the reader views that person, situation or event. Look at the following cartoon.

Notice that although "little Billy" has "the latest" computer system, he is playing with pots and pans. The cartoon above tells you that sometimes young children enjoy playing with simple, common objects and are not always interested in the more expensive items that their parents buy for them. Generally, cartoons contain few, if any, words, but if you study the characters' surroundings or expressions, you should be able to understand the cartoonist's message.

Practice

Study the following cartoon and then answer the questions.

1. What special products and equipment are shown on the man's side of the garden?

_____

_____

2. What special products and equipment are shown on the children's side?

_____

_____

3. How do the plants on the children's side of the garden compare to the plants on the man's side of the garden?

_____

_____

4. What is the cartoonist's opinion of special garden products and equipment?

_____

_____

5. In the cartoonist's opinion, what does it take to have a successful garden?

_____

_____

 **Application**

Maria Montgomery is in favor of a new highway being built from the northern suburbs into Boston. Every day, Ms. Montgomery spends two extra hours going to and coming from her job because of traffic jams on the present highway.

George Portland owns a drive-in restaurant on the present highway. He and other business owners along the highway are against any plans for a new highway because the new road would bypass their businesses.

Draw two cartoons. The first should be a cartoon from Ms. Montgomery's viewpoint. It should show what will happen if the new highway is *not* built. The second cartoon should be from Mr. Portland's viewpoint. It should show what will happen if the new highway *is* built.

Extension

Think about your opinion on the role of professional sports in our society. Then draw a cartoon that shows your opinion. Your cartoon should try to influence a reader to agree with your opinion.

- *Comprehension*—main idea/details, reality/fantasy, fact/opinion, cause/effect, problem/solution, paraphrase/summarize, inferences/conclusions, comparisons, referents, bias, judgments
- *Thinking*—analysis, synthesis, evaluation, visualization, prediction, questioning, monitoring
- *Spelling*—sound/letter patterns, words
- *Writing*—narrative, expository, descriptive, persuasive, functional, creative, writing process, writing conventions
- *Language*—grammar, usage
- *Literature*—story structure, author's craft, genres
- *Listening*—attentive, informative, critical, appreciative
- *Study skills*—text aids, graphic aids, text structure, note-taking, categorizing, outlining, summarizing

In short, most skills and strategies taught in any form, using any medium, can be reinforced (via the teach-practice-apply-extend method) with a supplementary workbook.

Getting Published

The cycle of workbook publication begins when the author forms an idea for a workbook series. The idea may spring from a special instructional interest, from a research finding, from an observed need in the marketplace, from an inspiration, or from a desire to "build a better mousetrap." Once the idea exists, the other steps in the cycle are fairly straightforward: develop a proposal, submit it to a publisher, enter into contract negotiations, and sign the contract.

It is critically important to develop a first-rate proposal. Your ideas may be great and the eventual workbook series might be exactly what the world needs, but unless the proposal is clear, complete, and articulate, development may never proceed. Publishers will make preliminary decisions about the feasibility, desirability, and marketability of the proposed work on the basis of the proposal's organization and appearance as well as its content. Proposals also help publishers form impressions about the author's ideas, style, carefulness, and effectiveness. You must take the time to prepare the proposal properly.

Proposal formats and contents will vary (some publishing houses have proposal guidelines), but any good proposal must include these elements:

- *Statement of purpose.* Begin by stating explicitly what the proposed series intends to do.
- *Statement of need.* Then describe the need in schools for this series.
- *Description of content.* This section should contain the series' scope and sequence, a tentative table of contents, and sample lessons for different levels.
- *Author's background.* Include a vita as well as a description of your qualifications to write this series. Samples of previously published works may be included.
- *Recommended timeline.* This part should include an estimate of how long it will take to write each book in the series, when work can begin, and when you expect to finish.
- *Competitive analysis.* In this section, describe similar works that are currently on the market and illustrate how the proposed series differs.

If a publisher is interested in the proposal, a representative will arrange a meeting to discuss the project. During this meeting, deadlines are agreed to and a publication schedule is developed. Also, lesson modifications are ironed out, and such issues as permission responsibility, art specifications, manuscript conventions, galley review responsibility, and contract details are resolved.

The contract will spell out titles, authorship, delivery schedules, financial matters (e.g., grants, advances, and royalties), and other business and publishing details. It is rare for a workbook series author to receive a grant to underwrite manuscript preparation. Small advances against royalties are usually awarded and are paid at the completion of milestones along the way (e.g., signing the contract, submitting each book). Royalty rates for workbook series vary widely. Most are between 4 and 6 percent of net sales; occasionally they are as high as 8 or 10 percent. The contract also should specify how the publishers will recoup the advance from the royalty payments and when royalties are paid.

Writing the Series

Writing a workbook series, like writing anything else, is demanding. Because of the typically tight deadlines specified in a workbook contract, it is imperative that the author stay on task and not fall behind. When writing a workbook manuscript, it makes sense to follow the usual steps in any good writing process: prewriting (planning and organizing), writing, revising, proofreading, preparing the final manuscript, and delivering it to the publisher. Publishers typically expect delivery of a workbook manuscript every month or two. If, for example, each workbook has 36 four-page lessons, the author would need to complete one lesson—four pages—every day or two. Each lesson requires all the writing process steps. In addition, artwork must be specified and, when applicable, permission information prepared.

The author has other tasks as well. Edited manuscripts must be reviewed and corrected, galley proofs must be reviewed, and sometimes page proofs must be checked. Thus, at the same time you're writing a new lesson, you are also reviewing things you wrote a month or two ago. In addition, the author must occasionally meet with the editors to work out problems and to consult on layout, design, and artwork.

The job of authoring a workbook series takes a lot of time, and that time must be spent in a continual and regular way. Tasks cannot be saved up until spring break or the next free weekend. Most successful workbook authors block out daily chunks of time, often very early in the morning or late at night if they have other daytime jobs, in order to stay on schedule. It is a big undertaking, and one might wonder why anyone would want to do it.

Benefits of Workbook Authorship

Certainly the biggest benefit of writing workbooks is the satisfaction of knowing that you are having a direct impact on teaching and learning. An elementary school teacher may reach only 25 or 30 students a year. An education professor may reach 100 prospective teachers in that time. On the other hand, a good workbook series may be used by thousands of practicing teachers each year. The author's potential impact on learning is tremendous.

Workbook authors know that the results of their labors are valued by the teachers who use the series (even if not by armchair critics). Teachers are extremely busy professionals, and they welcome help with planning, organization, and instruction. They wish to attend to individual students, but they cannot work with each small group at the same time. They want to use instructionally sound materials, but they rarely have the time to construct the materials themselves. As a result, many teachers appreciate the support provided by a good workbook series.

The workbook author enjoys other benefits while planning and writing the series. The work has focus, which enables the author to concentrate on developing materials that treat a topic in depth. Authors and their editors do most of the work themselves. Unlike a basal series development team, which may comprise hundreds of people (authors, editors, planners, designers, researchers, freelance writers, artists, graphics specialists, and marketing managers), a workbook team is small. One or two authors, one or two editors, and one or two artists and design people do the job. Thus, workbook authors know the series is *theirs*. Every word has been written by the author (with the helpful skills of the editor). An additional benefit is the project's duration. Compared with other kinds of published works, time between the acceptance of a proposal and the publication of a series is relatively short, sometimes only a year or so. A feeling of accomplishment comes more quickly.

The workbook author's potential impact on learning is tremendous. ■ ■ ■

Finally, workbooks can have remunerative rewards. In some ways, royalty authors are like farmers: they take big risks with no assurance of any gains. Like farmers, authors make great investments of time, talent, and treasure, and they must wait for a long time to learn whether their hard work has paid off. Numerous factors affect that payoff, including many that are not under their control and that have nothing to do with the quality of their work. The farmer's plantings may yield no produce, and the author's series may find no buyers. But when a workbook series does well, just as when growing conditions result in a bumper crop and market prices are favorable, the financial rewards can be good. And unlike farming, which repeats the cycle every year, royalty income can continue long after the initial investment was made.

Workbook authors need to develop a thick skin, but keep some softness, too, so they can savor the pride and joy of authorship.

Reference

Reading in the content area, level F. (1989). Cleveland, OH: Modern Curriculum Press.

CHAPTER TWELVE

Publishing Computer Software

Marguerite C. Radencich

■ ■ ■ ■

In this chapter, Radencich describes the process of conceiving of, writing, and publishing educational micro-computer software. She begins by discussing the advantages and disadvantages of packaging an idea as software. The discussion is guided by her experience as both the author of numerous journal articles and the coauthor of two highly successful computer programs in reading vocabulary and comprehension. After discussing the process of developing and circulating a proposal and securing a publisher, Radencich describes how to develop the software and manual by working with a team.

If authoring commercial reading programs ranks low on the prestige meter in educational circles, as Pikulski states in his chapter, then writing educational software is even farther down on the list. Nonetheless, it does have its rewards. If you are considering turning an idea into software, you will find little in the way of how-to books. Certainly, many of the suggestions mentioned in this book for other types of writing apply to software as well. However, some tips are unique to software, and it is these tips that will be discussed here.

Advantages and Disadvantages of Packaging
Your Idea as Software

Perhaps you have unsuccessfully made the rounds of publishers with an idea for a workbook and have thought of turning that idea into software instead. Or maybe you see software publishing as more profitable, since computers have received more grassroots support from both students and teachers than any other type of technology. Perhaps you feel that software will allow options not available with other media.

Regardless of your motivation, you are considering writing software for computers. You hear that no technology in education has sparked such intense competition for the educational market among so many areas of private enterprise. On the other hand, you hear that software development is expensive and risky and often only marginally profitable. How should you decide?

Choosing software as the medium for your idea presupposes that the computer can tackle a particular learning objective at least as well as other media can. This point is particularly important in the language arts, where the use of workbooks on screen has been so vehemently criticized. If it is desirable for students to write creative responses rather than select multiple choice answers, and if student responses need to be judged, the computer is not your medium. The computer has limited answer-judging capability for widely ranging, constructed responses. Similarly, if the goal is for students to read extensively, the poor resolution of print on computer screens again makes this technology a poor choice. A compromise, of course, is to combine the use of print with the use of software. For example, with the popular "Carmen Sandiego" software programs (Broderbund, 1985, 1986, 1988), students must use almanacs or travel guides to solve whodunits.

Publishing software is not easy. The programming isn't the problem (you can always work with a programmer); the hard part is meeting high standards of instructional and technical quality. This chapter will outline the steps needed to produce high-quality products.

Is there an abundance of high-quality software on the market today? Opinions vary widely. What is certain is that there are endless software programs to choose from. Thus, breaking into the software market is a difficult proposition. Promising avenues include software that:

- can be adapted to local needs such as preparation for state testing or integration into existing curricula;
- comes in languages other than English (note changing U.S. demographics with an ever-increasing Hispanic population);
- is tailored for students in federally funded programs such as adult education (vocational, business, and adult basic education), exceptional student education, and Chapter 1;
- includes comprehension aids (background information, paraphrasing, summaries, pronunciations of difficult words, glossaries);
- emphasizes cooperation; and
- enhances meaningful activities such as writing (word processors) and researching (databases).

Finding a Publisher

Developing a Proposal

The procedures for developing a software proposal are similar to those described in this book for other types of writing. Choose your objectives carefully. You want an idea whose content is new but not too new, or publishers may back off. Write your proposal in outline form and include (1) a rationale with clearly stated objectives; (2) a description of your proposed type of program (e.g., drill and practice, simulation, tutorial, instructional game, problem solving), required hardware, unique features, and program elements; (3) a statement of subject area, topic, grade levels of the intended learners, and specific areas of cognitive learning; (4) appropriate market; and (5) background of the author(s). Include concrete samples of your product. Some publishers will want to see a prototype on disk. Others feel that developing more than the concept, an outline, and some sample text is a waste of time since anything more specific would have to be redone to match their specifications.

When listing the unique features of your proposed program, be sure to start and end with particularly strong points. Make certain that you outline ways in which you make use of the computer's capabilities. While it may not be desirable to use all of these capabilities (for instance, sound or moving graphics may interfere with the purpose of your program), you certainly will want to use at least some of the computer's unique potential, such as the capability to provide immediate, responsive feedback and automatic data collection.

Circulating Your Proposal

The process to follow for getting your software proposal to publishers is similar to that followed for other commercial materials. Look at software directories and catalogs, and visit computer laboratories, software stores, and exhibit booths at conventions to see what kinds of products different companies favor. (The list of educational software publishers in the Appendix is a good starting point.)

Choosing a publisher must involve thorough researching of publishers' products. Some companies sell inexpensive software that focuses on one reading skill. Others prefer more comprehensive packages. However, because these packages are costly and more likely to be copied illegally, many publishers shy away from them. As with any product, it is important to select a publisher that has an established market in your area but that does not market a product quite like the one you envision. This is especially important for software publishers, many of whom dominate particular segments of the market.

Software publishing is still very much a cottage industry, so in addition to the publishing giants there are many small companies to choose from. Publishers differ in what they want. Comprehensive programs that can be networked for classes to use without students having to handle the disks would appeal only to large companies; simpler programs would interest both large and small companies. Some companies are proprietary about developing their products and will extensively modify what you submit; others will publish what you send them almost unchanged. Look also at publishers' marketing techniques. Some publishers market mostly through catalogs and maybe through conventions. Others go farther by having consultants actively market their products.

With software it is permissible to submit a proposal to several publishers simultaneously. Before submitting a proposal, call publishing houses or talk to their consultants at conferences to find out the name of the person to whom you should write. You are much more likely to get attention that way than through a "to whom it may concern" letter. One way to attract attention to your proposal is to use letterhead that is a color other than white. Back up letters with phone calls or personal contact.

The advice of Teacher Support Software President Lynn Domenech is to "package your idea in ribbons and bows." In other words, you must sell your product the way any successful salesperson does. Publishers may not have the time to figure out that your idea is worth pursuing. Thus, you must present your idea in a way that is simple and catchy. Tell publishers why they need your product. Finally, without making yourself obnoxious, do keep after publishers who don't respond.

Signing a Contract

Getting to the point of signing a contract can be costly. Aside from minor outlays for postage, photocopying, and phone calls, you may have to travel to make a face-to-face presentation. As with any contract, you will want to consult a lawyer, preferably one with software contract experience. Talk to acquaintances who have published similar materials to get an idea of the reasonableness of the contract's terms. Issues of disagreement obviously must be resolved. You may have to educate the publisher about the pedagogical rationale of some elements of your program. Your publisher may have to educate you about market realities.

Developing Your Product

Once your proposal is accepted and you have signed a contract, the real work begins.

The Software

There is no single set of generally accepted guidelines for writing software. Authors should, however, keep in mind the International Reading Association criteria for selecting nonprint media for the reading curriculum (Table 1).

Table 2 presents additional recommendations, framed in the form of checklist questions, for evaluating or planning the development of software. These recommendations are drawn from various sources (Balajthy, 1989; Cohen, 1983; Eisele, 1983; Jay, 1983; Wallace & Rose, 1984). Only those items not covered either by the Association's criteria or by the suggestions given earlier in this chapter are included. Recommendations are categorized according to educational content, presentation, interaction, and teacher use. It is, of course, not possible to include all positive elements in one program. However, all should be considered in the planning stages.

Table 1
International Reading Association Criteria for Selecting Nonprint Media for the Reading Curriculum

Print media include printed materials in books, pamphlets, magazines, or newspapers. Nonprint media include any other means of conveying information, including television, radio, computer, music, games, audiotape, film, videodisk, videotape, and cable TV.

1. Materials shall support and be consistent with the general educational goals of the school district.

2. Materials shall contribute to the objectives of the instructional program.

3. Materials shall be appropriate for the age, social, and emotional development and interests of the students for whom the materials are selected.

4. Materials shall present a reasonable balance of opposing sides of controversial issues so that students may develop the practice of critical reading and thinking. When no opposing side of an issue is currently available, the nature of the bias will be explicitly discussed and explained to the students.

5. Materials shall provide a background of information that will enable pupils to make intelligent judgments in their daily lives.

6. Materials shall provide a stimulus for creative reading, writing, listening, and thinking.

7. Material shall reflect the pluralistic character and culture of society. Materials shall foster respect for women, minority groups, and ethnic groups.

8. Material shall be of acceptable technical quality, including clear narration and synchronized pictures and sound.

9. Materials should be selected on the basis of their aesthetic quality, providing students with an increasing appreciation of the world around them.

10. Materials should encourage affective responses and further humanistic concerns.

Approved by the International Reading Association Board of Directors, May 1984.

Table 2
Software Development Checklist

Educational Content

☐ Is the information planned, sequential, and original?

☐ Is the level of difficulty consistent for the concepts and vocabulary presented?

☐ Does the program encourage recall of prior learning?

☐ Is the program compatible with other instructional materials? Does it provide for retention and transfer of learning to other events?

☐ Is the content sufficient to warrant the amount of teacher and student time?

☐ Is remediation differentiated from review?

☐ Does the program include pretests?

☐ Does it have evaluation components, including frequent questioning?

Presentation

☐ Is curriculum material logically presented and well organized?

☐ Are all the facts accurate? Is the use of spelling, grammar, and language precise?

☐ Does the software have quick response time and loading time?

☐ Does it present randomly generated items?

☐ Does any sound used enhance instruction without being distracting?

☐ Do the graphics enhance instruction? (Are the graphics clear, related to the text, and relevant for the users' age and ability level?)

☐ Does the use of color or other visual features enhance instruction?
  • Is important information emphasized with special characters, boxes, windows, underlining, blinking words, enlarged text, color, or arrows?
  • Does color use agree with habitual denotations—red for stop, green for go?
  • Have you avoided using too many different colors or "hot" colors (purple, orange, green)? (Hot colors are a particular problem when there is a high density of small print on the screen.)

☐ Does the software make use of mnemonics? (For instance, does it use a "b" rather than a nonmeaningful command for "begin"?)

☐ Is the screen display clear and easy to read (double spacing, sufficient space between words, use of upper- and lower-case letters, avoidance of right justification, one idea [one to two sentences] on screen at a time)?

☐ Are the menus descriptive?

☐ Does the program avoid "scrolling" or adding a line of print at the top or bottom of a screen when another line in the opposite position is deleted? (It is easier for a reader to "turn the page" forward and backward on the screen.)

☐ Is there a score display?

☐ Does the program have a "help" option?

☐ Does it safeguard against students "crashing" and having to restart the program (perhaps with erroneous inputs)?

☐ Can users exit and reenter where they left off? (This is particularly important with programs that run longer than 15-20 minutes. An alternative is to provide rest breaks.)

☐ Is the packaging designed for component parts (e.g., are there enough teacher's manuals for the number of grade levels covered in a package of material)?

☐ Does the program provide an emotionally healthy learning environment (e.g., without violence or sarcasm)?

☐ Is the presentation motivating and challenging? Does it encourage the learner to want to repeat the experience? (The motivation should be more than just the novelty of the computer experience or the interactiveness of the program; it must fit both the learner and the material being learned.)

Interaction

☐ Does the teacher have control over the level of difficulty, the speed of presentation, and the selection of program parts? (At the least, programs should allow more time for harder items—e.g., inductive questions—and less time for easier items—e.g., multiple choice questions.)

☐ Can the user correct entries?

☐ Can the user tell the computer when to display the graphic (to avoid having to concentrate on graphic and text simultaneously)?

☐ Does the software use prompts in the event of long computer delays so that users know they are to wait?

☐ Is there fading of cues and prompts that help students answer questions correctly?

□ Is a wide range of appropriate responses accepted (including those with either capital or lowercase letters and those with incorrect spacing)?

□ Does the software give intermittent reinforcement with meaningful praise?

□ Do errors elicit an error message with an explanation, a suggested action, and room for a response?

□ Does the program respond differently to different user answers (e.g., different responses for errors based on lack of attention to a medial vowel as opposed to a final consonant)?

□ Does it give personalized responses?

□ Is the feedback confirmational, motivational, and instructional?

Teacher use
□ Is the program effective without teacher monitoring?

□ Can the teacher modify the program to fit individual needs?

□ Are alternative learning opportunities suggested or provided for?

□ Does the program have a data trail to permit monitoring of each learner response (e.g., data from the learning situation, diagnosis and prescription recommendations, or reports on student progress)? If this process is too cumbersome, it will defeat the purpose of saving teacher time when individualizing instruction.

The Manual

We have all seen too many sketchy software manuals. Fortunately, an increasing number of software publishers are hiring writers with backgrounds in education and liberal arts, rather than programming, to prepare software manuals. Picture a teacher without much time examining a software program and flipping through its manual. Because first impressions are lasting ones, it doesn't hurt to have a manual that looks attractive and useful. The following tips will help you write a useful, appealing software manual:

- Incorporate information from your proposal into the manual.

- Indicate the necessary teacher qualifications for using the product and make sure the writing is neither too technical nor too simple for the intended audience.
- Describe the necessary support system needed for effective technical and pedagogical use of the product. What peripherals are needed? How much teacher involvement is required?
- Write concise sentences and use familiar vocabulary. List any acronyms, computer terms, or other words students will need to be taught.
- Include a detailed table of contents and a complete index. If appropriate, include a summary for each section, a tutorial for hands-on experience, and a quick reference section (maps, tables, equations, figures, diagrams) that can help minimize memory demands.
- Pay attention to physical factors that enhance text considerateness (e.g., white space, highlighting of subtitles or key concepts).
- Indicate a typical setting (individual, small team) and span of time for program use.
- Provide specific instructional activities to integrate the software into the curriculum.
- Summarize field testing procedures and results.

The Design Team

With some types of writing, you may tend to work alone unless you see a distinct advantage in working with a particular coauthor. But developing software by yourself would be a little like trying to produce a basal reader series alone. Producing software is not really a question of authoring but one of instructional design. Authoring implies writing and publishing; instructional design implies (1) using a model and a written design document, (2) taking a team approach to development, and (3) seeking formative review and evaluation.

Using a model and a written design document. Software design should be based on a model of how children learn. Using such a model will result in a product that emphasizes instruction rather than one that is technically flashy but instructionally ineffective. The instructional design should include written statements of goals and objectives, a learning map, a description of learning events, and flowcharts and storyboards—all *before* programming begins.

All parties involved in software development must have knowledge of both computers and education. ■ ■ ■

This type of development takes time; estimates of the amount of time needed to develop 1 hour of software range from 100 to 200 person hours or more (Roblyer, 1982b). But working without such a plan can be even more time consuming in the long run. Roblyer asserts that a systematic approach is critical and that it does not deter creativity. She cites as an example the director George Lucas, who insisted on a storyboard for every scene he shot in *Raiders of the Lost Ark*.

Taking a team approach to development. Producing software isn't as simple as saying to a programmer, "I write the content, you do the programming." Nor is programming like adding special effects after a movie has been shot. The Figure shows an optimal team relationship for developing software. A key feature is that the learner is at the center of all decisions. Design principles are built into the developmental process; thus, they will operate on the structure of the message, and not only on its form.

Radencich

Figure
Software Development Team Interactions

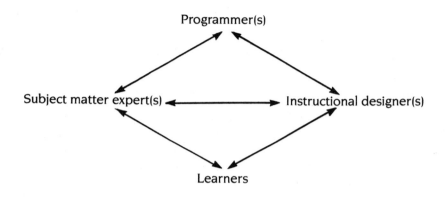

Programmer(s)

Subject matter expert(s) ←——————→ Instructional designer(s)

Learners

This model allows the programmer to see what the designer and subject matter expert have in mind and to offer alternatives that can improve on their ideas. All three professionals decide on the machine(s) for which the software will be written; different machine capabilities will be a factor in some instructional design decisions. A person may wear more than one hat in this relationship, but it is unlikely that one person will be effective in all three positions. Even if one person had the professional capability, an individual cannot eliminate biases and build quality control. Nor can an individual working alone compete in quality with well-funded professional organizations whose livelihoods depend on the effectiveness of their products.

All parties involved in software development must have knowledge of both computers and education; otherwise communication problems cause friction and hinder progress. This type of problem is illustrated in a remark by one data processing director: "You educators can never tell me what you want, but when I develop something for you, you can sure tell me what you don't want!" (Roblyer, 1982a).

Other problems that can hamper team effectiveness include working with team members separated by great geographical distances, setting the design in concrete before all draft materials are developed, treating programmers as less important members of a team, and (conversely) leaving all technical decisions up to the programmers. In the past, when the educational software industry was largely dominated by textbook companies, problems arose when development teams had little or no knowledge about software. Textbook publishers had to learn that software development meant more than simply turning a team loose on a project and giving them a deadline.

Formative review and evaluation. Formative evaluations may occur at a number of stages in the development cycle. Before programming begins, experts may review the design and concept. During programming, use of sample screens while letting one target person walk through the program can be helpful. Some authors make paper screens in a variety of sequences so they can see the responses that would result without doing any programming.

The most sophisticated form of evaluation is actual field testing. Students from the target group try out first-draft materials (software and documentation) either individually or in small groups. Later these materials are tested under regular classroom conditions with teachers who are trained in the process. With this type of testing, it is important to observe users as they are trying out the software. The requirement for field testing is by no means universal. Truett (1984) says that most publishers do not perform field tests because they are not convinced that the cost is warranted. Intense competition may, however, change this picture.

Finishing touches. Even after the evaluation stage, you are not finished. This is the time for making changes or enhancements suggested by the formative evaluation. It is also the time to run a final check. There is no substitute for sitting down in front of the computer and reviewing every screen in the program and then double checking to make sure no inconsistencies exist between your software and your manual.

Conclusion

As I reread this chapter, I note that I haven't strictly adhered to all of these suggestions in writing my own software. So don't despair if these guidelines seem unreasonable. But as the software market gets tighter—and this tightening goes beyond the rapidly increasing sophistication of the past decade—going by the rules is becoming increasingly important. If you start off with a good idea, all the hard work and careful preparation may pay off. And once you break into the software market it is easier to publish the second time around.

References

Balajthy, E. (1989). *Computers and reading: Lessons from the past and the technologies of the future.* Englewood Cliffs, NJ: Prentice Hall.

Broderbund. (1985). *Where in the world is Carmen Sandiego?* [Computer software]. San Rafael, CA: Broderbund.

Broderbund. (1986). *Where in the U.S.A. is Carmen Sandiego?* [Computer software]. San Rafael, CA: Broderbund.

Broderbund. (1988). *Where in Europe is Carmen Sandiego?* [Computer software]. San Rafael, CA: Broderbund.

Cohen, V.B. (1983). Criteria for the evaluation of microcomputer courseware. *Educational Technology, 23*(1), 9-14.

Eisele, J.E. (1983). Selecting courseware. *Educational Technology, 23*(5), 37-38.

Jay, T.B. (1983). The cognitive approach to computer courseware design and evaluation. *Educational Technology, 23*(1), 22-25.

Roblyer, M.D. (1982a). Developing computer courseware must be easier than some things. *Educational Technology, 22*(1), 33-35.

Roblyer, M.D. (1982b). Instructional design of courseware: Good news and bad news. *Educational Technology, 22*(3), 36-37.

Truett, C. (1984). Field testing educational software: Are publishers making the effort? *Educational Technology, 24*(5), 7-12.

Wallace, J., & Rose, R.M. (1984). A hard look at software: What to examine and evaluate (with an evaluation form). *Educational Technology, 24*(10), 35-39.

Recommended Readings

Balajthy, E. (1989). *Computers and reading: Lessons from the past and the technologies of the future.* Englewood Cliffs, NJ: Prentice Hall. This is a current and comprehensive book on the topic.

Blanchard, J.S., Mason, G.E., & Daniel, D. (1987). *Computer applications in reading* (3rd ed.). Newark, DE: International Reading Association. The chapter on evaluating and developing reading software includes a list of review sources. Also of interest are the extensive annotated bibliographies and the chapter on predicting the future.

Cohen, V.B. (1983). Criteria for the evaluation of microcomputer courseware. *Educational Technology, 23*(1), 9-14. Cohen's list of minimal standards was compiled over a period of 1 year by a review team of two instructional designers, two subject area specialists, and two technical experts.

Reinking, D. (Ed.) (1987). *Reading and computers: Issues for theory and practice.* New York: Teachers College Press. The text offers reviews of research and descriptions of specific computer-based projects. Topics include artificial intelligence, the technology of print, computer analysis of written materials, eye movement technology, and computer speech.

Roblyer, M.D. (1983). Five steps to instructional design disaster. *Educational Technology, 23*(2), 33-34. This article provides tips on teamwork for software development.

Selfe, C. (1985). *Computer-assisted instruction in composition: Create your own.* Urbana, IL: National Council of Teachers of English. This book gives how-to tips for creating software related to writing instruction.

Appendix
Educational Software Publishers

These addresses and telephone numbers are reasonably correct as of March 1991 but are subject to change.

Active Learning Systems
1053 LaMoree Rd.
San Marcos, CA 92069
(619) 744-8308

ActiVision
3885 Bohannon Dr.
Menlo Park, CA 94025
(415) 329-0800

Addison-Wesley
Jacob Way
Reading, MA 01867-9984
(800) 447-2226

Advanced Computer
 Tutoring
4516 Henry St.
Pittsburgh, PA 15213
(412) 621-5111

Advanced Ideas
2902 San Pablo Ave.
Berkeley, CA 94702
(415) 526-9100

American School Publishers
(Macmillan/McGraw-Hill)
PO Box 408
Hightstown, NJ 08520-9377
(800) 843-8855

Apple Computer
20525 Mariani Ave.
Cupertino, CA 95014
(408) 996-1010

Barron's Educational Series
250 Wireless Blvd.
Hauppage, NY 11788
(800) 645-3476

Baudville
5380 52nd St., SE
Grand Rapids, MI 49512-9765
(616) 698-0888

Beagle Bros.
6215 Ferris Sq., Ste. 100
San Diego, CA 94121
(800) 345-1750

Blue Lion Software
90 Sherman St.
Cambridge, MA 02140
(617) 876-2500

Borland International
4585 Scotts Valley Dr.
Scotts Valley, CA 95066
(800) 255-8008

William K. Bradford
310 School St.
Acton, MA 01720
(800) 421-2009

Brainbank
175 Fifth Ave., Ste. 2460
New York, NY 10010
(212) 777-7035

Britannica Software
345 Fourth St.
San Francisco, CA 94107
(415) 546-1866

Broderbund Software-Direct
PO Box 12947
San Rafael, CA 94913-2947
(800) 521-6263

Buchan Publications
PO Box 7218
St. Petersburg, FL 33734
(813) 526-9121

Claris
5201 Patrick Henry Dr., MS C56
Santa Clara, CA 95052
(800) 544-8554
(408) 727-8227

Classroom Consortia Media
  Gemstar
1 Edgewater Plaza
Staten Island, NY 10305
(800) 237-1113

COMPress
(See Queue)

Compu-Teach
78 Olive St.
New Haven, CT 06511
(800) 448-3224

Conduit
University of Iowa
Oakdale Campus
Iowa City, IA 52242
(319) 353-5789

cpi software
145 E. 49th St.
New York, NY 10017
(212) 753-3800 (call collect)

Creative Publications
5040 W. 11th St.
Oak Lawn, IL 60453
(800) 624-0822

Cross Educational Software
504 E. Kentucky Ave.
Ruston, LA 71270
(318) 255-8921

Davidson & Associates
3135 Kashiwa St.
Torrance, CA 90505
(800) 556-6141

D.C. Heath
(See William K. Bradford)

Designware
(See Britannica Software)

Didatech Software
3812 William St.
Burnaby, British Columbia
Canada V5C 3H9
(604) 299-4435

Discis Knowledge Research
NYCC PO Box #45099
5150 Yonge St.
Toronto, Ontario
Canada M2N 62N
(800) 567-4321

DLM
One DLM Park
Allen, TX 75002
(800) 527-5030

Educational Activities
1937 Grand Ave.
Baldwin, NY 11510
(800) 645-3739

EduSoft
PO Box 2560
Berkeley, CA 94702
(800) 338-7638

Electronic Arts
1820 Gateway Dr.
San Mateo, CA 94404
(800) 245-4525

EPYX
600 Galveston Dr.
Redwood City, CA 94063
(415) 368-3200

First Byte
3100 S. Harbor Blvd., Ste. 150
Santa Ana, CA 92704
(800) 523-8070

Focus Media
839 Stewart Ave.
PO Box 865
Garden City, NY 11530
(800) 645-8989

Gamco Industries
PO Box 310Y
Big Spring, TX 79721
(800) 351-1404

Gessler Educational Software
55 W. 13th St.
New York, NY 10011
(212) 627-0099

Grolier Electronic
Publishing
(See Houghton Mifflin)

Harcourt Brace Jovanovich
Southeast Region
Seventh Floor
Orlando, FL 32887
(407) 345-4300

Hart
320 New Stock Rd.
Asheville, NC 28804
(800) 654-8012

Hartley Courseware
(part of Jostens)
133 Bridge St.
Dimondale, MI 48821
(800) 247-1380

Holt, Rinehart & Winston
383 Madison Ave.
New York, NY 10017
(212) 872-2213

Houghton Mifflin
7055 Amwiler Industrial Dr.
Atlanta, GA 30360
(800) 241-9612

Human Relations Media
(See Queue)

HyperGlot Software
505 Forest Hills Blvd.
Knoxville, TN 37919
(800) 726-5087

IBM
1133 Westchester Ave.
White Plains, NY 10601
(800) 222-7257

Imperial International
  Learning Corp.
329 E. Court St.
Kankakee, IL 60901
(915) 933-7735

Intellectual Software
(See Queue)

Jostens Learning Systems
800 E. Business Center Dr.
Mt. Prospect, IL 60056
(800) 323-7577

K-12 Micromedia Publishing
6 Arrow Rd.
Ramsey, NJ 07446
(800) 292-1997

Knowledge Revolution
497 Vermont St.
San Francisco, CA 94107
(415) 553-8153

Koala Technologies
2699 Mt. Herman Rd.
Scotts Valley, CA 95066
(800) 562-2327

Krell Software
Flowerfield Bldg. 7, Ste. 1D
St. James, NY 11780
(800) 245-7355

The Learning Company
6493 Kaiser Dr.
Fremont, CA 94555
(800) 852-2255

Learning Lab Software
21000 Nordhoff St.
Chatsworth, CA 91311
(800) 247-4641

Learning Technologies
(See Merit Software)

Learning Well
(See Society for Visual Education)

Lightspeed Software
2124 Kittredge, Ste. 185
Berkeley, CA 94704
(415) 486-1165

Logo Computer Systems
330 W. 58th St., Ste. 5D
New York, NY 10019
(212) 765-4780
(800) 321-5646

Macmillan/McGraw-Hill
(See American School Publishers)

MECC
3490 Lexington Ave., N.
St. Paul, MN 55126-8097
(800) 228-3504
(612) 481-3500

Mentor Learning Systems
PO Box 710116
San Jose, CA 95171-0116
(408) 358-7807

Merit Software
13635 Gamma Rd.
Dallas, TX 75244
(800) 238-4277

Micro Power & Light
12820 Hillcrest Rd., Ste. 219
Dallas, TX 75230
(214) 239-6620

Microsoft
16011 NE 36th Way
PO Box 97017
Redmond, WA 98073-9717
(800) 227-4679

Midwest Publications
PO Box 448, Dept. 17
Pacific Grove, CA 93950
(800) 458-4849

Milliken Publishing
1100 Research Blvd.
PO Box 21579
St. Louis, MO 63132
(800) 643-0008

MindPlay
13130 N. Dodge Blvd.
Tucson, AZ 85716
(800) 221-7911

Mindscape
(See Society for Visual
    Education)

National Geographic Society
Dept. 5397
Educational Services
Washington, DC 20036
(800) 368-2728

Pelican Software
(See Queue)

Prentice Hall
Sylvan Ave.
Englewood Cliffs, NJ 07632
(201) 592-2745

Polarware
521 Hamilton St.
Geneva, IL 60134
(312) 232-1984

Queue
338 Commerce Dr.
Fairfield, CT 06430
(800) 232-2224

Random House
(see American School Publishers)

Roger Wagner Publishing
1050 Pioneer Way, Ste. P
El Cajon, CA 92020
(800) 421-6526

Scholastic Software
PO Box 7502
2931 E. McCarty St.
Jefferson City, MO 65102
(800) 541-5513

Scott, Foresman
1900 E. Lake Ave.
Glenview, IL 60025
(800) 554-4411

Sierra On-Line
PO Box 485
Coarsegold, CA 93614
(209) 683-6858

Silver Burdett & Ginn
250 James St.
Morristown, NJ 07960-1918
(800) 848-9500

Simon & Schuster
Gulf & Western Bldg.
1 Gulf & Western Plaza
New York, NY 10023
(800) 624-0023

Tom Snyder Productions
90 Sherman St.
Cambridge, MA 02140-9923
(800) 342-0236

Society for Visual Education
1345 F Diversey Pkwy.
Chicago, IL 60614-1299
(800) 829-1900

The Software Toolworks
One Toolworks Plaza
13557 Ventura Blvd.
Sherman Oaks, CA 91423
(818) 885-9000

South-Western Publishing
5101 Madison Rd.
Cincinnati, OH 45227
(800) 543-7972

Spectrum Software
75 Todd Pond Rd.
Lincoln, MA 01773
(617) 893-9130

Spinnaker Software
(See Queue)

Springboard Publishing
(See Queue)

Styleware
5250 Gulfton, Ste. 2E
Houston, TX
(713) 668-0743

Sunburst Communications
101 Castleton St.
Pleasantville, NY 10570
(800) 628-8897

Teacher Support Software
1035 N.W. 57th St.
Gainesville, FL 32605-4483
(800) 228-2871

Techbyte
217 S. Union St.
Burlington, VT 05401
(800) 361-4993

Techware
PO Box 151085
Altamonte Springs, FL 32715
(407) 695-9000

Terrapin
400 Riverside St.
Portland, ME 04103
(207) 878-8200

Radencich

Timeworks
444 Lake Cook Rd.
Deerfield, Il 60015
(800) 323-7744

Walt Disney Personal
  Computer Software
10316 NW Prairie View Rd.
Kansas City, MO 64153
(800) 423-2555

Weekly Reader/Optimum
  Resource
10 Station Pl.
Norfolk, CT 06058
(800) 327-1473

J. Weston Walch
321 Valley St.
PO Box 658
Portland, ME 04104
(800) 341-6094

Wings
1600 Green Hills Rd.
PO Box 660002
Scotts Valley, CA 95067-0002
(800) 321-7511

World Book
Merchandise Mart
Station 13
Chicago, IL 60654
(800) 323-6366

P A R T   **T H R E E**

*Publishing
Textbooks
and
Professional
Books*

CHAPTER THIRTEEN

Publishing College and Professional Texts

Hiram G. Howard

Susanne F. Canavan

In this chapter, Howard and Canavan—both principals in Christopher-Gordon Publishers—describe the process of publishing college and professional texts from the editor's perspective. They begin by distinguishing college textbooks from professional books. Next they describe the steps an author must take to secure a publisher and have a proposal accepted. Also included are guidelines for conceiving of a writing project, identifying prospective publishers, preparing and submitting a prospectus and sample chapters, negotiating a contract, writing the first draft, revising the manuscript, and assisting in the book's production.

■ ■ ■ ■

There is something of a mystique attached to publishing, something special about being published. On the one hand, publishing is a business like any other; on the other hand, it involves many creative individuals in the venture of transmitting knowledge—the product of the human mind—and transforming it into the medium of print. While the author's role is basically a solitary endeavor, the publisher's task is much more public, requiring cooperation, accuracy, a separate store of knowledge, and the ability to orchestrate numerous disparate elements.

College and professional text publishing shares some of this mystique and a bit of the magic, yet it is firmly grounded in more practical matters. What is this field all about? A college textbook is designed to be one of many pedagogical tools the professor uses to instruct students. If the text is meant for use in an introductory-level course, it should provide students with the basics of a particular discipline. If the text is for an upper-level or graduate course, there is an assumed knowledge base, and the content and presentation are quite different. Books intended for practicing teachers have further distinctions.

In trade publishing, books are produced for any number of reasons, but mainly because editors think enough people will read them to keep the companies in business. Educational publishers respond to audience needs by producing books for existing courses and established disciplines. Since college courses rarely use just one text, the types and number of texts published depend on how the courses are taught, the number of courses on a given topic, and the number of students taking these courses each year. In short, the markets usually are well defined, and the total universe of possible users is fairly predictable.

When editors consider proposals for new textbooks, a number of factors come into play: overall student enrollment, the number of schools that might adopt such a text, the number of students graduating in different areas, and so forth. Another factor is the percentage of the market an editor thinks a new book will capture. All this sounds rather speculative, but the system does work to a greater or lesser degree (depending, like most things, on the accuracy of information that fuels it).

College versus Professional Texts

A college text is written with a particular course in mind. Content and length are determined by what is generally taught in this course in colleges across the country and how many weeks the professor has to cover necessary course information.

Professors are unlikely to use a text that requires them to change how they normally teach a course, that is missing important information, or that includes too much information for them to cover in a single term.

What professors do want are books that reflect the latest theory and research in their fields. They also want books that will appeal to their students, especially in their undergraduate courses. This means that a lively writing style, a particularly effective pedagogy, or unusually creative use of illustrations may be decisive factors in swaying a professor to use one book rather than another. Naturally, publishers know all this, which means that if you want to write a college text, you have to address each of these matters to their satisfaction.

Professional texts are aimed at a different audience—the practicing educator—and have a different intent. These readers have solid grounding in their disciplines; the professional text is designed to refine their knowledge, usually focusing on one particular concern.

While the market for professional texts is less strictly defined than that for college texts, market knowledge is still important. For this type of book, editors need to know how many teachers might purchase the book, the state requirements that might affect sales, and the current hot professional topics. Table 1 expands on the similarities and differences between college and professional text publishing.

Choosing the Type of Book to Write

Why choose one type of book over another? Writing any book-length work requires discipline. Text writing requires great knowledge of a familiar area and the ability to present it in an expected manner, perhaps with new insights. Professional text writing is highly focused. The author's intent is to give readers a new perspective on some aspect of their discipline. Readers of college texts go to them to gain knowledge; readers of profes-

Howard and Canavan

Table 1
A Comparison of College and Professional Texts

College Text	Professional Text
Intended for a specific course	Not necessarily course related
Parameters, content determined by existing courses and practice	No predetermined content; can focus on a specific topic
Little author flexibility	Great author flexibility
Huge markets in some courses	Markets frequently smaller
Stiff competition for market	Not as much competition; therefore, more chance of success
Riskier proposition; some professional risk if book fails	Little professional risk if book fails
Significant financial rewards possible	Modest financial rewards possible

sional texts want to know how best to use the knowledge they have.

What type of book is best for *you* to write? We can't answer that, but we can suggest the right questions to ask yourself about your ambitions and abilities. If you're not sure whether you're ready to write college or professional texts, we suggest that you stop now and take the self-test found in the Appendix at the end of the chapter.

The type of book you write depends largely on where you are in your career and your motives for wanting to write in the first place. Do you think you have something important to say about your discipline? Do you expect to make a lot of money by writing a book? Do you hope that publishing a book will earn you prestige or a promotion? Do you regard writing as a professional responsibility? What audience do you want to reach—your colleagues, practicing teachers, undergraduate students?

Your reasons for writing and your target audience will affect the type of book you choose, how you direct your writing efforts, the level of publishers' interest, and overall sales potential.

Once you have decided you want to write a college or professional text, you need to choose your target course or topic, the amount of time you can realistically devote to the project (i.e., how long it will take you to finish the book), and which publisher you would like to work with.

Thinking about your own work experience may help you focus on a topic. For example, have you experienced growing dissatisfaction with the texts you have used in teaching an elementary reading methods course? Have you developed a new method of presentation that seems to work well with your students? Has your line of research offered interesting perspectives on classroom practice or suggested new avenues for college instruction? Answers to these and other questions will help narrow the scope for the next part of the process, selecting publishers to approach.

Finding a Publisher

Choosing an appropriate publisher is more important than most people realize; the effort requires as much consideration as deciding what to write about. The right publisher may make the difference between the success and failure of the entire writing experience. Think about it: Do you want to spend 2 or more years of your life working on a book that ends up with a publisher only marginally interested in your topic or not equipped to sell your book to its target audience? Table 2 presents a series of possible questions you might ask about a potential publisher of your book.

You need to consider a number of publishers before selecting one, and we strongly advise you to submit materials to several simultaneously. Such side-by-side comparisons will give you a good indication not only of how interested various com-

Table 2
Questions to Ask When Considering Publishers

- Does this company frequently publish the kind of book I want to write?
- How long has the company published in my area?
- How do I rate the quality of the books the publisher has produced in my area? How do I regard the authors?
- Have I used any of this company's books in my own courses? What did I think of them?
- What is the company's reputation in my field?
- Have any of my close colleagues published with the company? How do they feel about their experiences?
- How does the company sell the type of book I want to write?
- How often do I see the company's sales representatives? Have the representatives been helpful and knowledgeable?
- Does the company regularly exhibit at national meetings?
- What sorts of advertising would my book get?
- Who would the editor be, and what is that person's experience?
- Would my book fit into the company's list?
- How many new titles in my area does the company publish every year? How many revisions?
- How stable is the company financially? Is it part of a larger organization? Has it experienced growth over the past few years?
- What have I recently heard about the company, either positive or negative?

---

panies are in your work but also of how they operate. (Note that while the simultaneous submission of a textbook proposal is acceptable, it is against accepted practice to submit an article simultaneously to two or more professional journals.)

Being a good person with a good idea is not enough to get a proposal accepted. Once you have narrowed down your list of

Table 3
Making a Positive First Impression
with a Prospective Editor

- Find out who the editor is. A simple phone call will do it. Editors don't like to get proposals addressed to predecessors who left the company 5 years ago.
- Make sure you have the company's current address. Forwarding orders do expire.
- Research other books on your topic; know their comparative strengths and weaknesses.
- Send a letter of inquiry first, briefly stating your book idea (no more than two pages at this stage) and asking for guidelines for developing a prospectus and table of contents. If you have written sample chapters, be sure to mention this. You usually will be asked to submit chapters for review unless the editor already knows you.
- You may want to follow up with a phone call. If you've spoken with the editor and your material is expected, you're already a step ahead of the pack.
- Your sample chapters should be substantive and showcase what you know best.
- Be sure to include a vita with your material.
- Don't send form letters with names filled in.
- Don't send an entire manuscript without first asking.
- Don't be too impatient. It may take an editor several weeks to respond to your submission. This is one reason that multiple submissions are a good idea.

possible publishers, you need to plan how you are going to sell them your book idea. Editors are busy; they travel a lot, and they are constantly immersed in paperwork. They may receive dozens of unsolicited proposals every week. Each proposal has about 30 seconds to make a positive first impression before being rejected or put into a short pile for further consideration.

How can you make sure your proposal gets more than a cursory glance? A little preparation here will go a long way. Ta-

Table 4
Things *Not* to Say to a Potential Editor

- Tell me what you want me to write. (You should already know what you want to write.)
- There's no book like this one; or, there are no other books for this course. (Perhaps nobody is interested.)
- All I need to do is expand my doctoral dissertation. (UGH!)
- All I have is this one-page outline, but I can have the book finished in 6 months. (Provided I have nothing else to do.)
- This book can be used in any course. (And, conversely, in none.)
- I haven't taught the course for several years. (So my information is probably outdated.)
- I have plenty of time to write. (The people publishers want to write books are invariably the busiest.)

ble 3 presents a brief list of steps you should take before sending your material off to any publisher. Table 4 lists some pitfalls to avoid when communicating with prospective editors.

The Prospectus as a Sales Tool

Before committing their companies to anything, editors generally need to see at least a prospectus and table of contents for the book you want to write. Unless you have already published successfully or are a recognized name in your field, you will probably have to submit sample chapters. But first let us go through the prospectus, your most important tool in selling a publisher on your project.

Remember that editors are more marketing and product managers than experts in your field, so your prospectus needs to focus on questions that concern them: market size, competition, outstanding features (sales benefits), and your qualifications to write the book. In our experience, prospective authors have the most trouble with defining the market, specifying the writing level, and assessing the competition. It is all too easy to reinvent the wheel, particularly in large markets that have many books. Authors must have a good sense of the overall market and the distinct segments that may exist in some areas. Sometimes authors lose sight of their readers and make false assumptions about their level of knowledge or what they will do with information from the book.

Drawing up a prospectus may help clarify several issues in your own mind, but at this early stage, everything should be quite fluid. By the time you get to serious writing, you should have answered most of the following questions to your own satisfaction (and, with luck, to the satisfaction of at least one editor). Typical components of a book prospectus follow.

Brief description.   What is your book about, and why are you writing it? If you think existing books are outdated, say so, but do it professionally and tactfully; many people probably still like those books.

Market.   Who is your audience? This is often the most difficult feature for an author to pinpoint and the place where most problems occur. Different audiences have different needs, not all of which are compatible or consistent.

Competition.   Are there other books like the one you're proposing? If so, describe them. If not, why not? Editors want to know the context in which you're writing.

Outstanding features.   Why does the market need another book on this topic? What differentiates your book from the others? This section is extremely important; be as specific as possible.

Apparatus.   What will make your book work as a learning tool? Why will professors want their students to use it? The second question relates to supplementary features such as end-of-chapter questions, illustrations, in-chapter boxes, outlines, and the instructor's manual.

Status of the work.   If you have a good idea, publishers want to know how quickly it can be turned into a salable book. Plan on 18-24 months to finish a manuscript if you're just starting; add another 9-12 months for production before the book is published. How faddish is your idea? The market may be gone by the time the book is done. Editors are always more interested in projects that are already well underway.

Length of the finished book. The length of your book should be comparable to the length of similar books. Editors are suspicious of books that are much longer or shorter than the present norm.

Vita. A vita helps establish your credentials for writing the book. Publishers like to minimize risk where they can. Your academic credentials help them establish your potential as an author who will deliver the goods. A successful writing record is helpful (although it does not always guarantee success). If you've published very little, you'll have to do a great deal to persuade a publisher that you can carry out a book-length project.

Table of contents. Your contents will not tell the whole story, but it will let publishers see in general terms how your book compares with existing ones. Usually, it is helpful to include an abstract for each chapter to let editors and possible reviewers know your planned approach. These annotated contents are particularly helpful if they accompany sample chapters since they provide a better sense of context.

Sample materials. Anyone can create an impressive outline; editors want to know if you can write and deliver on your promise. When selecting which sample chapters to write, choose substantive ones that show your expertise in the best possible light. Avoid introductory or summative chapters.

Getting the Best Possible Contract

So where does all this effort get you? If you know your topic and have put together a package of materials that is the answer to an editor's dreams, you may face the enjoyable dilemma of having to choose from a number of contract offers.

Every author hopes to have this luxury. Although greater competitiveness among publishers has made such choice more common, it does not happen in every case; much will depend on the kind of book you're writing. So while you should never immediately grab the first contract you're offered, neither should you keep a publisher dangling for months in the hopes of getting other offers. If you do receive more than one offer, the contract with the biggest numbers isn't necessarily the best. You need to compare all offers carefully.

A publishing agreement marks the beginning of a relationship between an author and a publisher that may extend over many editions and span decades. Many authors who signed contracts in haste regretted the move for years. Always remember that the agreement is the publisher's document, and it is understandably structured in the company's best interests. This is not to say that publishing contracts are devious or unfair, but you should be aware of what you are signing. You may not like everything you read, and while there are some things you might be able to change, others you cannot.

Table 5 summarizes some of the finer points of publishing agreements. Some of them make sense, such as the publisher having the right to make decisions regarding format, marketing, and price. Others are less clear, and some can be downright painful for unwary authors. You should read carefully any contract you receive. These are only general highlights. Contracts vary from publisher to publisher, and you may wish to consult with an attorney, but awareness is really your best negotiating tool.

The main points an author should focus on in contract negotiations are (1) a stipulated period of time for the publisher to reach an acceptance decision and to publish the book once it has been accepted, (2) a realistic manuscript delivery date with a reasonable grace period, (3) adequate funds to cover the cost of producing an acceptable manuscript, (4) protection against hidden costs, and (5) adequate earnings. Some publishers will

Howard and Canavan

Table 5
Publishing Agreements: Read the Small Print

A *contract may give a publisher the right to*:
- choose the format for your book
- determine how the book is marketed
- set the price for the book
- choose the title for the book
- grant subsidiary rights with or without compensation to the author
- terminate the agreement if the manuscript is not delivered on time
- terminate the agreement if the manuscript is not acceptable
- revise the book for a new edition without the author's permission
- reduce royalty payments if sales fall below a certain level

A *contract may obligate an author to*:
- deliver a manuscript of a certain length by a certain date
- deliver a manuscript in a specific form
- be responsible for reading galley or page proofs
- pay for alterations of typeset text (above a certain percentage)
- pay for any permissions to use materials from other sources
- pay for any artwork in the book
- refrain from writing a competing work for another publisher

A *contract generally does* not:
- specify when the publisher will decide whether to accept the final manuscript
- state when a manuscript will be published
- prevent the publisher from selling the project to another company

respond to these points on a case-by-case basis, while others have standard policies. Either way, what concessions they make will depend largely on how much they want your book.

Acceptance and Publication

Probably the most critical element of any publisher's contract is the issue of acceptability for publication. What does this mean? Can the publisher still decide to reject your manuscript after the contract has been signed? Yes, it can. There are many legitimate reasons for refusing to accept a completed manuscript—for example, if it contains inaccurate information, is poorly written (even after extensive revisions), or is badly organized. On the other hand, publishers also reject manuscripts for reasons that have nothing to do with quality. For example, a publisher may decide at any time to limit, or even end, its commitment to a certain field. Or it may discover that your project requires unanticipated financial commitments, or that the market for the project has changed dramatically, making the book obsolete even before it gets into print.

Publishers do not like to sign books and then not publish them; it is demoralizing and expensive, and it can jeopardize future signings in related fields. On the other hand, no publisher wants to commit itself irrevocably to publish a book 2 or 3 years down the road. As we all know, a lot can happen in that time. For one thing, markets change constantly. This flux is both an asset and a liability. On the one hand, it means a constant need for new or updated products; on the other, it means you can completely miss a market or see it dissolve in front of you.

While all of this may be understandable from the publisher's position, it leaves the author in the vulnerable position of being committed to writing a manuscript that has no guarantee of being published. What can an author do? You may be able to get the publisher to add a paragraph to your contract setting a date by which the publisher should decide whether to accept your manuscript for publication. The paragraph should stipulate that if the publisher fails to reach a decision by that date, the rights to the manuscript will automatically revert back to the author.

The intent here is obvious. If a publisher gets into difficulties of one sort or another (and it happens), the author should not have to stand by with an aging manuscript until the company sorts itself out. The author should have a legal right to take the manuscript to another publisher if the current publisher cannot reach an acceptance decision within a reasonable amount of time.

You should try to get a similar paragraph inserted for publishing the book within a specified amount of time after acceptance, again with reversion of rights to the author if the deadline passes. Publishers may be reluctant to add these paragraphs, but there are precedents, so be sure to at least ask for such clauses.

Delivery Date

Many authors misunderstand what the delivery date represents. This date is when, by contract, the publisher is supposed to receive the complete, final manuscript with all its various elements. Naturally, a publisher is going to want to set the date for sooner rather than later.

There are a number of elements to consider when figuring out a delivery date. The first is that writing is going to take longer than you thought. You need to take both your professional and your personal situation into consideration. What are your teaching and advising responsibilities? Do you have other duties in your department? How long does it normally take for you to write a chapter or an article? Where do you do most of your writing? If at home, have there been any major changes— new baby, return of older children, new job, illness—that may affect your normal routine?

Do not let the publisher pressure you into agreeing to an unrealistic delivery date. If you are starting from scratch, it will take you at least 18 months to finish the manuscript, plus several additional months for reviews and revisions. These are only estimates; your writing time will be influenced most by the type of book you are writing.

On the other hand, you don't want too leisurely a writing schedule because you run the risk of missing your market entirely. There is no guarantee that a market will be there when your book is, but significant change is more likely over a longer period of time.

Be sure to set yourself intermediate dates for completing portions of the manuscript. Time has a way of evaporating, and while the final delivery date may seem a long way away, you don't want to be in the position of writing half the manuscript in 3 months. You can write only so quickly.

You should try your best to deliver your manuscript on time, especially if you are looking for guarantees of acceptance and publication dates. If you are late delivering the manuscript, you may seriously jeopardize your agreement. Publishers may tie their dates for acceptance and publication to your delivery date, so think these things through carefully.

Expense Funds

Ideally, a publisher likes to sign contracts that cost them no money up front. This means that they prefer authors to bear all the expenses of writing a manuscript up through publication. The result is that you might not see any reward for your efforts until several years after you sign the contract, assuming your first royalties are not eaten up by permissions fees or artwork charges. From the author's point of view, it makes sense to ask for expense funds.

Generally, expense funds cover manuscript preparation, permissions, and artwork. If publishers want you to work for them on speculation to produce a manuscript they won't guarantee they'll publish, it seems only fair that they should pay these expenses. Permissions and artwork come later; your immediate concern is how to pay for producing the physical manuscript.

Manuscript preparation. A publisher should provide enough money for you to produce an acceptable manuscript without having to dip into the family cookie jar to buy paper, make phone calls, or pay for word processing. If you have to foot the bill for these payments, your manuscript's progress may be slowed for purely financial reasons, and its future may be threatened if there's a significant delay.

What are the actual costs of producing a manuscript? How much money should you ask for? Your biggest expense will be getting the manuscript down on paper. Expect to pay around US$4 a page for word processing and printing; if your manuscript is projected to be around 400 pages, you're already looking at the healthy sum of $1,600. And don't forget revisions, copying, postage, and phone bills.

The right publisher may make the difference between success and failure. ■ ■ ■

Permissions. After word processing, the biggest expense is usually permissions fees, or the price other publishers charge for your using their copyrighted material. As you know, it is difficult for an educator, scientist, or any writer whose field is learning and knowledge to write without drawing on the material of other researchers and scholars. Permission is required (fees may be charged) for longer quotes, extensive paraphrasing, and reproduction of charts, graphs, and illustrations. The individual fees may not be high, but for a whole book they can add up to hundreds or even thousands of dollars.

Permissions fees usually are not due until your book has been published, so you may not be overly concerned with them in early stages. The usual case is for the publisher to pay the fees all at once and deduct them from your royalties. It's all relatively painless, but you should be aware that the money ultimately is coming out of your pocket.

The publisher's stance that permissions fees should be the author's responsibility stems from a desire to keep overall permissions costs down. The argument is that you will be more careful in your use of other writers' material if you have to pay for it. This generally holds true, but since it is almost impossible to write a textbook or professional book without using material from other sources, the publisher should bear at least some of the costs (particularly for textbooks, which usually require more permissions).

Artwork. Authors need to pay special attention to artwork clauses. Most contracts state that the author bears the cost of art preparation. Again, the logic is that the more authors have to pay the more careful they'll be with costs, but many books require artwork to be competitive in their markets. If a publisher truly wants your book to be competitive, the editor should add a paragraph to your contract saying that the publisher will pay up to a certain price for a specified amount of artwork (with the author picking up the cost for anything over that amount). If the original figure is equitable and the artist comes in on budget, you're okay. You may still have some art charges to pay, however.

Using photographs is not a way around art charges unless you happen to be a very good photographer. Even then, there are costs involved; and if one of your photos doesn't work out and a commercial photograph has to be substituted, you'll be liable for photo permissions charges, which in many cases cost more than artwork. You need to make sure your editor explains all these details *before* you sign any contract.

Hidden Costs

Some costs don't necessarily come up at contract time but may appear later on your royalty statement. Most likely your contract will contain a paragraph regarding the cost of author's alterations. Author's alterations are any changes in the typeset galley proofs that are not corrections of typesetter errors. Most publishers will pay the cost of changing a certain percentage of the text—usually around 10 percent, a fairly generous figure. The cap is intended to prevent authors from rewriting their books in galleys or page proofs. Making changes at that stage is expensive and may delay the publication of your book. After typesetting, any changes you make should be confined to absolutely crucial information.

Unexpected art charges may also crop up, particularly when tearsheet material (usually figures from other sources that can be reproduced without redrawing) has to be modified in some way (usually type replacement). Not a whole lot can be done about these charges, and they may never arise, but you should be aware of them and ask that you be informed if such charges are necessary.

Earnings

We have heard many prospective authors say, quite earnestly, that they didn't particularly care how much money their books might make; it was more important to them that the books be published. We applaud this dedication, but we should mention that many of these authors were later pleasantly surprised by some rather healthy royalty checks. Our point is that you can be committed to making a contribution to your field and still think about earnings from your book.

Earnings, or royalties, are paid to authors out of the money the publisher receives from sales of their books. Percentages vary with the type of book, the author, how much the company wanted the book, and how the book is sold, among other factors. Royalties are one of many costs involved in producing a book. Ironically, it is one area where publishers have a large degree of control.

In recent years, because of escalating costs for paper, printing, and postage, many publishers have been trying to control overall costs by holding firm on royalties. We can appreciate this, since authors earn a royalty on each book sold, while publishers see no profit until they've sold enough copies to recover the money spent publishing the book in the first place. And while some books comfortably exceed their sales projections, publishers may never recover their costs on others.

Royalty rates may range from 10 to 18 percent for multiple copy sales (i.e., to bookstores for resale) and 5 to 8 percent for single copy sales (to individuals, usually through the mail). The publisher will want to sign you for the lowest possible rate for your type of book, and, of course, you'll want the highest possible rate. It is impossible to be specific here about what constitutes a "good" royalty rate since so many variables come into play. You should focus on what seems fair given the circumstances.

If a publisher insists on a very low royalty rate and won't be budged, try to get a sliding scale so that if your book sells more than a specified number of copies, the rate increases. The idea is that once the publisher's costs are covered and the book is earning some profit, the author should reap part of the reward. This seems an equitable arrangement; the lower initial rate allows the publisher to recover its costs more quickly without blocking the author from sharing in the book's success.

Other Points in the Contract

As we noted earlier, contracts generally give publishers the right to choose the format (e.g., book size and length, cover design, typeface, binding, use of color) and to market the book as they see fit. Presumably, these areas are where the publisher's expertise comes into play; however, if a publisher is trying to cut corners, these are where the cuts come. There is no way publishers can give authors choice or approval in these matters, but certainly they can keep you informed about any decisions before publication. And it doesn't hurt editors to ask authors if they have any strong preferences or if they like or dislike certain types of covers.

Two clauses that sometimes concern authors have to do with revised editions and noncompetition. The clause on revisions, which allows publishers to revise with or without the author's consent, is virtually unenforceable. The author's professional community is relatively small, and it would be very awkward for a publisher to recruit someone to do a revision against the author's wishes—or to sell the book to that community if the revision did get done. If a book is successful, it is in the author's interest to revise it in a timely fashion. It really is easier the second time around, and if you're too involved in other things, coauthors are the answer.

Also virtually unenforceable is the clause that states authors cannot write other books that would compete with the work under contract. To our knowledge, publishers rarely if ever accuse an author of this. We know of several instances where authors have written books for different publishers that could be seen as competing, but in fact they coexist side by side. The closest this ever came to being a problem was when one of us asked an author to adjust his revision schedules for two similar books so they would come out in different cycles.

Remember, although some clauses in the standard publishing agreement can be changed, others cannot. You need to decide which issues are important to you and which ones are not. Most of all, you need to be very aware of the contract terms and use that awareness to your best advantage. Most publishers are not going to point these things out to you. *Let the signer beware.*

In conclusion, we wish you the very best in your publishing endeavors and hope that your dealings with publishers are positive and worthwhile. What we have told you is based on our experience and knowledge; others may have very different perspectives. We hope that by applying what we have shared with you, you'll find the thrill of getting your first royalty check equal to the thrill of holding a copy of your first book.

Appendix
Are You Ready to Write a College or Professional Textbook?

This brief test may help you judge your potential in this field by looking at the criteria publishers use to evaluate prospective authors. Of course, many factors will affect an editor's evaluation of your writing potential, but the following questions focus on the first things publishers look for. We've put the scoring criteria at the end of the test so you won't be biased.

1. How old are you?
   - (a) 35 or under
   - (b) 36-40
   - (c) 41-45
   - (d) 46-50
   - (e) Over 50

2. If you teach at the college level, what is your present rank?
   - (a) Associate professor with tenure
   - (b) Full professor with tenure
   - (c) Assistant professor
   - (d) Lecturer
   - (e) Graduate student

3. If you're a classroom teacher, what is your level of education?
   - (a) Ph.D.
   - (b) Working on a Ph.D.
   - (c) Master's degree plus additional coursework
   - (d) Master's degree
   - (e) Bachelor's degree

4. If you hold a doctorate, where is it from?
   - (a) A nationally recognized school in your discipline
   - (b) One of the largest schools in your discipline
   - (c) A large state school
   - (d) A small state school
   - (e) Other

5. During the past 5 years, how many articles have you published in refereed journals?
   (a) 15 or more
   (b) 10-14
   (c) 5-9
   (d) 1-4
   (e) None

6. What types of work have you published? (Circle more than one if applicable.)
   (a) Other textbooks
   (b) Chapters in textbooks
   (c) Journal articles
   (d) Book reviews and newspaper articles
   (e) None

7. What presentations have you made during the past 5 years?
   (a) More than two papers a year at two or more different national meetings
   (b) One paper a year at two or more different national meetings
   (c) More than two papers a year at two or more different regional or local meetings
   (d) One paper a year at one or more regional or local meetings
   (e) None

8. Have you taught at a level other than college?
   (a) Yes
   (b) No

9. For how long have you been teaching the course your proposed text covers?
   (a) Over 5 years
   (b) 2-4 years
   (c) 1-3 years
   (d) This is the first time
   (e) I haven't taught the course for a year or two

10. For what type of course is your proposed book designed?
    (a) A required course for all students
    (b) A required course for all students majoring in a particular discipline
    (c) An elective
11. What type of text do you wish to write?
    (a) A core text required for a particular course
    (b) A supplemental text for a required course
    (c) A text suitable for more than one course
    (d) A supplemental text for an elective course
    (e) A book for no specific course, but one that would be useful for all students in a particular discipline

To score the self-test, give yourself four points for every (a) answer, three points for every (b), two for every (c), one point for every (d), and zero for every (e). The higher your score, the greater your author potential in publishers' eyes.

Writing Professional Books; *or*, The Second Stone

Wayne Otto

■ ■ ■ ■

In this chapter, Otto provides an author's-eye view of writing college textbooks and professional books. Relying on words of wisdom provided by his fancied friend and seer, Fats Grobnik, and conjecturing about the kind of college textbook humorist Dave Barry might write, Otto presents a whimsical but insightful view of the constraints facing textbook authors. He writes from experience, having authored a number of college reading textbooks. He argues that when publishers take a market-driven approach to textbook writing, they get texts that are bland, passionless, humorless, and pedantic—as he calls them, basal readers for adults.

"**A**nd why beholdest thou the mote that is in thy brother's eye, but perceivest not the beam that is in thine own eye?" Thus admonished Fats Grobnik after I'd told him what I thought I'd have to say on the topic of publishing professional books —particularly textbooks—from an author's point of view. Then he added, "That's Luke 6:41, in case you've forgotten your Bible passages from Sunday School."

Fats was right on target, as usual. His words stung me all the more because they reminded me of an essay on the topic of textbooks that I'd read just a few weeks earlier. It was one of the "This View of Life" columns Stephen Jay Gould writes each month for *Natural History* magazine (January, 1988). As a textbook writer about to discuss certain limitations and flaws of textbooks and the people who write them, Gould reminded his readers—and himself—that "the wisdom of our culture abounds with mottos that instruct us to acknowledge the faults within ourselves before we criticize the failings of others" (p. 16). He cited not only the cliché about what pots and kettles call each other but also certain sayings of Jesus, including the very one Fats Grobnik used to instruct me.

Apparently, though, Fats didn't think I'd been chastised enough by his initial blast, so he let me have the other barrel. He told me, "He that is without sin among you, let him first cast a stone." And then, after pausing to let me contemplate my shortcomings, he finished up his dazzling display of total recall. "John 8:7," he said, with what I judged to be his idea of a sweet Sunday School smile.

Everybody who knows him knows that Fats Grobnik is forever criticizing the fishing techniques of all the muskie anglers in the whole of northern Wisconsin and Minnesota combined. But I personally know that he himself never caught a muskie over 16 inches, so I thought he was being a little smug about ignoring eye beams and casting first stones. Still, I knew that deep down my good buddy had my best interests at heart. Not only that, but if we got to talking about Fats' faults, we'd never get back to talking about what I was there to talk about in the first place.

So I Sunday School smiled right back at Fats and said, "Bless me, father, for I have sinned." Then, while we talked some about the beams in my eyes, I commenced to contemplate casting the second stone.

Eye Beams and Stones

Like Fats said, when it comes to criticizing the faults and shortcomings of textbooks and their authors, I'm in a poor position to be beholding motes in the eyes of others. As coauthor of several textbooks, my faults and shortcomings in that area are obvious and, from the perspective of my own maturity, profound. I acknowledge them; I have no excuses.

I'll not cast the first stone.

Even if I were inclined to, there's no opportunity. The first stone's already been cast—many times over—by the reviewers of books and the critics of schools and schooling. So I'm in the exposed but enviable position of occupying a glass house where all the windows are already broken. I get to throw the second stone.

Like I told Fats, I don't mean to throw that stone in an ill-spirited, destructive way. It's just that I think a little friendly stone throwing from a guy in a splintered glass house might be better than a lot of heavy pontificating about how to write the world's greatest textbook.

A Clearer View

Actually, it wasn't just Fats' admonishments that put me into an antipontifical frame of mind. After reading *Dave Barry's Guide to Marriage and/or Sex* (1987) a couple of months earlier, I'd got to thinking about what a whimsical guy like Barry might do if he turned his awesome talents to writing a textbook about reading. One thing led to another, and finally I wrote an essay (Otto, 1988) about the book I imagined Barry would write if he ever did take up this subject. I want to share with you some excerpts from that essay because in the course of preparing it I came to a clearer view of what I really think about textbook writing than I'd ever come to before.

This, I imagined, is what Barry would title his tome and how he would introduce it:

> With a whimsical touch we might get something like *Dave Barry's Guide to Reading and/or Dyslexia*, complete

with introductory remarks especially for academics— people like you and me, who are charged with the enormously complicated responsibility of teaching everybody to read everything they see regardless of whether they are ready or not and whether they know much of anything else or not—as contrasted to real people, who think they can learn to read simply by figuring out what the squiggles say and deciding how much of that makes sense to them (Otto, 1988, p. 271).

There's more to that introduction, but I need to break in here to say that after just one paragraph of imagining from the shoulders of Dave Barry, I had already gained an important insight about textbook writing. First, you pick a title that titillates and promises. Then you continue titillating by making it clear that you are about to address issues that are so enormously complex that hardly anybody grasps the very complexity of them. Then you extend the promise by hinting that your book does in fact address those complexities in ways heretofore unimagined by scholars in the field. Finally, having established the fundamental point that you are the world's foremost authority on the topic, you assure the reader that you've managed somehow, in spite of all that erudition, to cling to your common touch:

The basic problem, Barry might say, is that people who teach reading make a big deal out of learning how, even though people who learn how generally claim that how they did it was by doing it. And he would continue by pointing out that efforts to solve the problem have consisted mainly of articles in scholarly journals and in grocery store checkout counter magazines that have the following general lineup of articles:

- Effects of Four Treatments on Three Groups of Fifth Grade Readers
- Effects of Three Treatments on Four Groups of Fifth Grade Readers

- New (named after the authors) Test Proves 50 percent of Third Graders Read Below Grade Level
- New (named after some city or state) Test Proves 50 percent of Third Graders Read Above Grade Level
- Effects of Frank Brain Damage on the Meta-cognition of Male Third Graders Named Jason
- Two Headed Child Learns Analytic and Synthetic Phonics at Same Time
- World's Fastest Reader Exposed as Dyslexic (Otto, 1988, pp. 271-272).

And, of course, there must be an admonishment that success in implementing the book's advice requires hard work on the part of the reader—just in case things don't work out as promised:

> Then he would wrap up the introduction with a thoughtful word of advice before you get started: You cannot be a successful reading teacher just by reading this guide. For the teaching to succeed, there must be a learner who is willing to work. Work, work, work, that's the key. Endless, constant, extremely difficult, unproductive work (Otto, 1988, p. 272).

Finally, there must be another reminder of the timeliness and the depth of scholarship unleashed in the book:

> Also, he would conclude, there will be hard times along the way. Awful, terrible, horrible times. Which is why the guide includes helpful advice such as in Chapter 6, where the term dyslexia is introduced and the concept of using the term to describe and explain every type and degree of reading failure is discussed, accompanied by full-color diagrams of the occipital lobe and first person testimonials by leading brain surgeons and billionaire dyslexics (Otto, 1988, p. 272).

Then there's the actual content of the book. I imagined Dave's book would start with a chapter addressed to parents, even though the book was clearly intended for teachers. I realized that this approach would accomplish what all publishers want their authors to do first and foremost: address the widest possible audience, thereby expanding the sales potential even if it means meandering away from the main thrust now and again. Here's how Dave's chapter would go:

Chapter 1. For Parents: How to Find Somebody to Teach Your Child Phonics and Eventually to Read Actual Books Who Is Not a Total Jerk

This chapter, I think, would start with a self-scoring survey designed to help parents develop a psychological profile of the ideal reading teacher. Parents would be directed to pick the phrase that completes the sentences below:

Training

The person who teaches reading to my child should be:

1. A Harvard Ph.D. with big bucks in research grants and contracts.
2. The owner or principal stockholder of a nationally franchised tutorial service.
3. Able to read third grade basal texts at the frustration level or better.

Professionalism

The person who teaches reading to my child should:

1. Own a complete set of $1/64$ life size pewter figurines of members of the Reading Hall of Fame.
2. Proudly carry the platinum life member card of the Fail-Safe Reading-by-Rote Society.
3. Hold an honorable discharge from military service.

Sensitivity

The person who teaches reading to my child must:

1. Be certified as a master hugger by the Leo BusGAGlia School of Sincerity.
2. Find inspirational messages in all of my child's experience stories.
3. Refrain from laughing out loud at mispronunciations of multisyllabic words.

Intelligence

The person who teaches reading to my child should be smart enough to:

1. Recite titles of all the chapters in the *Handbook of Research on Reading*.
2. Explain the meaning of a test score that falls in the sixth stanine.
3. Name the vowels.

Scoring: Add up the numbers by your answers and check the chart:

If your answers total...	Your ideal reading teacher is...
1-8	A full professor at MIT
9-12	Selling aluminum siding in Great Falls
13	A paid subject in a learning disabilities study

With the matter of what to look for in a reading teacher fully explained, the rest of the chapter would be devoted to such important matters as getting your child into as many conflicting special programs as possible, how to help your child score high on standardized reading tests by random guessing, and getting your child out of special programs (Otto, 1988, p. 272).

Having disposed of the supplemental segments of the buying public with a few well chosen words, Barry would get on to more weighty matters (i.e., concepts explained in language nobody understands). This would, of course, reassure all the serious readers of the book—the hard line professionals like you and me—that Chapter 1 was merely a minor excursion to address a pressing but unmet need and that the rest of the book would be your basic scholarly (and mostly incomprehensible) stuff. The next five chapters would go like this:

Chapter 2. Making the Most of Background Factors, No Matter What
What you'd have here would be an extremely scholarly and comprehensive discussion of how to place the blame for poor reading performance on genes and chromosomes, nuclear waste, junk food, seasickness, and strabismus.

Chapter 3. Phonics
This is where you'd get into the fine points of the great debate between reading people who say you've got to be able to figure out words before you can read books, paragraphs, or sentences and reading people who seem to be wanting to say something else but can't quite figure out what. Of couse there would be a glossary of technical terms like *digraph* and *schwa*.

Chapter 4. Comprehension
Now, with all the easy stuff out of the way, Barry could get right down to explaining What Reading Is Really All About. What reading is really all about is *understanding* what all those words that get sounded out *mean*. Naturally, there would have to be a long, technical/philosophical discussion about whether *understanding* means what the author meant, what the reader guesses, or what the teacher has arbitrarily decided. And important technical terms like *metalinguistic* would be sort of defined, more or less.

I'd rely on Barry to behave like any responsible pedagogue by offering no sensible advice whatsoever on whose meaning it is that's important, why that's important in the first place, or how to help a reader look for whatever it is that *meaning* turns out to mean (Otto, 1988, pp. 272-273).

I have to break in here with another insight. What you've got to do as an author is get the issues out so that your readers can more or less see what they are. At the same time, you've got to be careful not to offend any possible buyers of your book by taking a clear stand on what these issues really amount to or by suggesting any straightforward ways to address them. This is all based on careful, scientific market analysis, which must be right because the people who do it get paid big bucks.

Chapter 5. Study Skills

Having discharged the major obligation of any reading guide writer, namely by obscuring the meaning of *meaning* and by rendering comprehension incomprehensible, Barry could get down to the practical stuff—study skills. Study skills are what you use when you try to guess what the teacher thinks is important in your textbook and will put on the exam. There are, of course, many important study skills; so it's a lucky thing that most of them can be represented by acronyms that spell out cute words or sayings like GLITCH, SPOOF, RACK UP, or FLUNK.

What teachers must do is to teach as many of these cute routines as possible so as to keep students from using any one of them long enough to find out it doesn't work. Or the teacher could just come right out and say that anything that isn't talked about in class won't be on the test.

Chapter 6. Dealing with Dyslexia

We need a chapter on this topic because it's in the title, but it's hard to guess what a whimsical guy like Barry would say. Most of the really funny stuff has already been published in scholarly tomes (Otto, 1988, p. 273).

At first I was a little disappointed by what I imagined about Chapter 6 on dyslexia, but after sober reflection I decided that not being able to imagine much of anything was probably okay. Not only has most of the funny stuff already been written, but almost anything that anybody could imagine has already been written. The lesson here is that every text must have at least one chapter that addresses a topic about which virtually nothing is actually known and then proceeds to summarize what is not known with copious footnotes, references, and personal anecdotes.

After Chapter 6, the rest of the book would be easy:

> There would have to be some more chapters to get up to the publisher's prime requirement: one chapter for each week in the semester. Since all the important topics have already been covered, it isn't important what the other chapters would be about. But I doubt that Barry could pass up such promising possibilities as ability grouping, programs for the gifted and talented, and competency testing (Otto, 1988, p. 273).

The insight gained from the imagined rest of the book is obvious, I guess, but I'll say it again because I like it: There's got to be as least one chapter for each week in the semester.

When I told Fats Grobnik about that last insight, he gave me a raised eyebrow, which always bothers me a lot. So I told him about the Instructor's Manual that publishers force their textbook authors to supply. That's the softcover thing that comes with the text; it includes a synopsis for each chapter (apparently to meet the needs of college instructors who are too stupid, too lazy, or too uninterested to read the actual book) as well as "assessment exercises," complete with answer keys (apparently for college instructors who have no idea what their course is about and no way to find the answers to questions raised by somebody who does).

That changed Fats' expression from a quizzical one to a say-it-ain't-so look. I sent him back a could-I-make-something-like-that-up look and commenced to sum up my thoughts.

Some Stones

What follows, then, is a summary of insights I've gained from my talks with Fats Grobnik, whose finger is on the pulse of America, my personal fantasies about what Dave Barry would say in a text about reading, and my extensive (and largely unsuccessful) experiences in coauthoring textbooks on reading. Interspersed among the insights are some stones—the ones I've already told you I feel free to throw because all the panes of my glass house have already been busted.

1. Textbooks on reading generally address the widest possible audience. A prefatory statement usually claims that the book addresses the needs of undergraduates, graduate students, teachers and other assorted school personnel, parents, and, at least occasionally, the entire literate population of the English-speaking world. Of course, this broad view, which is presented at the insistence of the publisher, renders it impossible for the authors or coauthors to say anything useful to any given segment of the audience.

2. Textbooks that present a broad view to a vast audience must also present nothing that could conceivably offend or alienate any group of potential buyers. This is why textbooks generally are devoid of passionate statements and personal points of view. Again, publishers are generally responsible for this lapse. When they insist on what they call "balance," what they get is insipidness.

3. Textbooks are also generally devoid of humor or anything that could in any way be interpreted as a light touch. I

can't blame the publishers for this one because I doubt that any humorous writing actually reaches them. Most academics view anything with a light touch as frivolous and unscholarly; consequently, most authors have had all the humor squeezed out of them before they get around to writing a textbook. In addition to insipid content, then, textbooks tend to have a pedantic style. The former may be from reason; the latter seems to be purely from habit.

4. In addition to being insipid and pedantic, your general, all-purpose textbooks on teaching reading tend to share another, related characteristic. This third characteristic defies neat labeling. What I'm talking about here is a whole set of conventions purportedly designed to enhance the "readability" of basic texts. Examples include never having more than two or three paragraphs between boldface subheads; showing lots of pictures; including endless, redundant examples; and writing at a formula-based fifth grade level. No real person would write like this, of course; such presentations come in response to publishers' demands.

Basic textbooks on reading have become basal readers for adults. ■ ■ ■

Now, I'm in favor of writing that is simple and direct, but I refuse to believe that simple and direct must be purchased at the price of writing by formula for readers who are presumed to be lazy and ignorant. I know lots of teachers who read real books. Often. And with understanding.

5. My insights so far—plus the Instructor's Manual phenomenon I mentioned earlier—lead me to a final insight: Basic

textbooks on reading have become basal readers for adults. Maybe everyone else has known this all along; maybe I've just been trying to deny the distressing, depressing reality of it. What I find most disturbing is that the development of professional textbooks appears to proceed with the same assumptions that guide the development of basal readers: that teachers can't be trusted to teach and that learners can't be trusted to become actively involved in their own learning.

I could go on like this at considerable length. I have an insight about the inclination of textbook authors to "borrow" from one another and thereby perpetuate aphorisms, fables, and myths that have little or no grounding in predictable and observable reality. And another about publishers' tendency to merchandise books, or sometimes authors, rather than ideas. And another about how users select textbooks in response to merchandising rather than any sensible analysis of audience and content. But enough; no need to continue making a point that may already be overmade.

Forces and Pressures

"The point is," I told Fats, "that people who aspire to write professional texts are going to be subjected to all kinds of forces and pressures that have little or nothing to do with writing a book that's worthwhile in any other than an economic sense."

"Does that mean you have nothing whatsoever to say to an aspiring author that would be constructive and useful?" Fats wondered.

I told him I guessed not, except that if people are aware of these forces and pressures, maybe they can resist them—or at least work around them.

Then Fats wondered if I was saying that we'd all be better off if there were no more textbooks. I told him, yes, if basic texts were going to turn out like basal readers.

But, I added, I think authors can still write really worthwhile books if they find good editors to work with. When Fats wondered what a good editor would be like, I told him it would be somebody who would let you write your book.

"So," said Fats, "what you're telling me is that your advice to aspiring textbook authors is to write what seems sensible, not necessarily what the market surveys call for."

That's what I was saying all right, but I didn't think at the time that I'd have the nerve to say it again. "Call me irresponsible," I told Fats.

Then Fats wondered if I ever planned to try another textbook, and I said never, no never. Fats asked skeptically, "What, *never?*"

And I said, "Well...hardly ever."

"Gilbert and Sullivan," Fats said, beaming. "HMS Pinafore."

References

Barry, D. (1987). *Dave Barry's guide to marriage and/or sex*. Emmaus, PA: Rodale.
Gould, S.J. (1988, January). The case of the creeping fox terrier clone. *Natural History, 97,* 16-24.
Otto, W. (1988, December). Wayne Otto's guide to reading and/or dyslexia. *Journal of Reading, 32,* 270-273.

Author Index

Subject Index

Note: "Mc" is alphabetized as "Mac." An "f" following a page number indicates that the reference may be found in a figure; a "t," that it may be found in a table.

Subject Index   ■

HISPANICS: software geared to, 171
HOLIDAY HOUSE: 109
HOMOGRAPHS: 157
HOMOPHONES: 157
HONORARIUMS: 38. *See also* Advances against royalties;
  Royalties
HORN BOOK, THE: 122
HORNE, FRANK: 107
HUMOR: in textbooks, 227-228

IDEA GENERATION: 44-45
ILLUSTRATORS: children's book, 118-119; minority, 119
INDEXES: reading program, 149; in software manuals,
  179
INFERENCES: conclusions and, 163
INSTITUTES: children's book publishing, 119; illustrator,
  118
INSTRUCTOR'S MANUALS. *See* Teacher's manuals
INSULT TO INTELLIGENCE (Smith): 88
INTERNATIONAL READING ASSOCIATION (IRA): 4, 21, 68, 77,
  143; editorial staffing policies of, 13-14; journals
  of, 4-7, 13, 41-42; listings of, 120, 139; member-
  ship in, 153; nonprint media selection criteria,
  174, 175. *See also Journal of Reading; Lectura y Vida;
  The Reading Teacher; Reading Today; Reading Research
  Quarterly*
INTRODUCTIONS, ARTICLE: 52f-53
IRA. *See* International Reading Association

JARGON: 27
JOHN BROWN'S BODY (Benét): xi
JONG, ERICA: viii
JOURNAL OF EDUCATIONAL PSYCHOLOGY: 3, 6, 14
JOURNAL OF MEMORY AND LANGUAGE: 14
JOURNAL OF READING: 4, 5, 41, 122; books highlighted
  in, 120
JOURNAL OF READING BEHAVIOR: 3, 14
JOURNALS: 122; editorial style of, 57-58; familiarity with
  31-39, 50; publication in, 2-66; selection of appro-
  priate, 49; themed, 34; as writer resource, 44. *See
  also* Practitioner journals; Research journals

KARL, JEAN: 126
KEEP THE LIGHTS BURNING, ABBIE (Roops): 126
KENNEDY, JOHN F.: 106
KING LEAR (Shakespeare): 25
KIRKUS: 122

LANGUAGE: 163; non-English software, 171; software,
  176t. *See also* Words
LANGUAGE ARTS: x, 29, 33-39, 42, 50, 122; profile of,
  31-32
LANGUAGE ARTS PROGRAMS: 146, 149, 151
LAYOUT, WORKBOOK: 166
LECTURA Y VIDA: 4
LEARNING MAPS: 180
L'ENGLE, MADELEINE: 115
LEVIN, LAURA: 22
LIBRARIANS: publisher-employed, 138-139, 150; and
  reading program development, 150; as writer
  resource, 111, 120
LIDDELL, KATHERINE: 102-103
LI PO: 107
LITERARY MARKET PLACE: 153, 154
LITERATURE: children and, 163; editing down of, 139
LONELINESS: writing and, 104, 112
LOOK-SAY METHOD: 9
LUCAS, GEORGE: 180
LUCK: writing and, 110

McELDERRY, MARGARET: 103, 108-109
McGUFFEY, WILLIAM H.: 130
MAGAZINES, WRITER: 108
"MAIN-IDEA-PEDE": 54
MANUAL OF STYLE, A: 7, 16, 37
MANUALS. *See* Teacher's manuals
MANUSCRIPT READINGS: 126-127
MANUSCRIPTS: mailing of, 59; preparation of, 37-40, 51,
  58, 70-71, 116, 123-124, 208-209; workbook,
  165. *See also* Submissions
MAPS: in software manuals, 179
MARKETING: of reading programs, 131. *See also* Advertis-
  ing; Salespeople; publishers'
MARKET RESEARCH: and reading programs, 151
MARKETS: 206; textbook, 197t, 202-203
MEDIA. *See* Nonprint media; Print media
MENUS, SOFTWARE: 177t
METACOGNITION: 87
MIDWEST SOCIETY OF CHILDREN'S BOOK WRITERS: 115
MINORITIES: respect for in nonprint media, 175t; in
  publishing/writing/illustrating, 119. *See also*
  Hispanics
MINORITY LITERATURE: 150
MNEMONICS: in software, 176t
MONITORING, READER: 163
MORROW (emergent literacy critic): 84
MS. MAGAZINE: 22
MULTIPLE-CHOICE QUESTIONS: in software programs,
  170, 177t. *See also* End-of-chapter questions
MUSIC: IRA selection criteria for, 175t

NATIONAL COUNCIL OF TEACHERS OF ENGLISH (NCTE): 4,
  39, 42
NATIONAL ELEMENTARY PRINCIPAL: 32
NATIONAL MINORITY PUBLISHERS EXCHANGE: newsletter
  of, 119
NATIONAL READING CONFERENCE: 21
NATIONAL SOCIETY FOR THE STUDY OF EDUCATION: 91
NCTE. *See* National Council of Teachers of English
NEW ADVOCATE, THE: 122
NEWBERY AWARD: 126
NEWSLETTERS: publishing in, 67-79; as writer resource,
  44. *See also* Bulletin, SCBW
NEWSPAPERS: classroom use of, 92; editorial style of,
  70; publishing in, 67-79; as writer resource, 44
NEWSPAPERS IN THE 7th GRADE: 92
NEW YORK HERALD TRIBUNE SPRING BOOK FESTIVAL: 104
NONCOMPETITION CLAUSE: 213
NONPRINT MEDIA: IRA selection criteria for, 175t. *See also*
  Audiotapes; Computer software, educational;
  Films; Games; Music; Radio; Television; Video-
  tapes
NOTETAKING: language arts related, 163
NO WAY OF KNOWING: DALLAS POEMS (Livingston): 105

OMAHA, NEB.: 104
ONOMATOPOEIA: 102-103
ORGANIZATIONS, PROFESSIONAL EDUCATIONAL: 21
ORIGINAL STORY PROBLEMS IN MATH: 92
ORTHOGRAPHY, CHINESE: 9-10
OTHELLO (Shakespeare): 18
OUTLINES: article, 48; language arts student, 163. *See
  also* Prospectuses, presubmission; Table of
  contents; as manuscript outline

PACKAGERS, BOOK: 118
PAGE PROOFS: author and, 165, 205t; author's altera-
  tions in, 211; journal, 38
PAPERBACKS: 125
PARAPHRASE: 163; in computer software, 171

Subject Index ■ 235

Subject Index